MASTERING LINKEDIN

Strategies for Professional Success and Networking Excellence

Teja Laveti

Title   :   Mastering LinkedIn : Strategies for Professional
               Success and Networking Excellence

Author   :   Teja Laveti

Edition   :   First (September, 2024)

ISBN   :   9788197785788

Published by

PRACHI
DIGITAL PUBLICATION

Regd. Add.: 254, Khuriyakhatta No. 10, Bindukhatta,
Lalkuan, Nainital - 262402, Uttarakhand, India
Website : www.prachidigital.com
E-mail : info@prachidigital.in
Phone : +91 976041 7980, +91 976041 8103

Printed by :

Manipal Technologies Limited, Bengaluru - 560001, Karnataka

ACKNOWLEDGEMENTS

Creating this book has been a collaborative effort, and I am deeply grateful to all who have contributed their expertise, time, and support. Firstly, I would like to extend my heartfelt thanks to the team at Prachi Digital Publication, whose dedication and hard work made this book possible. Your insights, editorial guidance, and commitment to excellence have been invaluable.

I am immensely grateful to the LinkedIn professionals and industry leaders who shared their success stories and provided practical insights that enriched this book. Your experiences serve as a beacon of inspiration for others. Special thanks to my professional network, whose collective knowledge and engagement have continually motivated me to explore new ideas and perspectives. Your feedback and interactions have been instrumental in shaping the content of this book. To my friends and family, thank you for your patience, understanding, and encouragement throughout this process. Your support has been my anchor, allowing me to focus and bring this project to fruition.

Lastly, I would like to acknowledge the readers of this book. Your pursuit of professional growth and mastery of LinkedIn is commendable. It is my sincere hope that the strategies and insights shared here will help you achieve your ambitions and build lasting, impactful connections.

INDEX

INTRODUCTION

Why LinkedIn Matters

In the digital age, networking and professional growth have transcended traditional boundaries. LinkedIn, the world's largest professional network, has emerged as a critical platform for individuals and businesses alike. This chapter delves into why LinkedIn matters, how it has transformed the professional landscape, and the myriad benefits of having an optimized LinkedIn profile.

The Evolution of Professional Networking

Professional networking has always been a cornerstone of career development. In the past, networking primarily occurred through face-to-face interactions, industry conferences, and personal referrals. However, the advent of the internet revolutionized the way professionals connect, collaborate, and advance their careers.

LinkedIn, founded in 2003, played a pivotal role in this transformation. It provided a virtual space where professionals from diverse fields could connect, share ideas, and explore opportunities. Today, LinkedIn boasts over 740 million users in more than 200 countries, making it an indispensable tool for career advancement.

The Power of a Digital Presence

Having a strong digital presence is no longer optional; it is essential. LinkedIn serves as an online resume, portfolio, and networking tool all in one. Here's why having a well-crafted LinkedIn profile is crucial :

1. Visibility and Reach : LinkedIn amplifies your visibility. Unlike traditional resumes that are seen by a limited number of recruiters, your LinkedIn profile is accessible to a global audience. This increased reach can lead to unexpected opportunities.

2. Professional Branding : Your LinkedIn profile is a reflection of your professional brand. It allows you to showcase your skills, experiences, and achievements in a manner that is both comprehensive and visually appealing.

3. Networking Opportunities : LinkedIn facilitates connections with colleagues, industry leaders, and potential employers. It breaks down geographical barriers, enabling you to build a robust professional network.

4. Job Search and Recruitment : For job seekers, LinkedIn is a powerful tool. Many recruiters use LinkedIn to find candidates, and many job postings are exclusive to the platform. A strong LinkedIn profile can significantly enhance your job search efforts.

5. Industry Insights and Learning : LinkedIn is a treasure trove of industry insights and professional development opportunities. Following industry leaders, joining professional groups and engaging with content can keep you informed and help you grow in your field.

Leveraging LinkedIn for Career Advancement

LinkedIn offers numerous features designed to help you advance your career. Understanding and utilizing these features can give you a competitive edge.

1. Profile Optimization : An optimized profile is key to standing out. This includes having a professional photo, a compelling headline, and a well-written summary. Highlight your experiences, skills, and endorsements to create a comprehensive picture of your professional journey.

2. Content Creation and Engagement : Sharing content, whether it's articles, posts, or comments, positions you as a thought leader in your field. Engaging with others' content also helps you stay visible and relevant.

3. Networking and Connections : Actively building and maintaining your network is crucial. Connect with colleagues, mentors, and industry professionals. Personalized connection requests and thoughtful messages can help foster meaningful relationships.

4. Job Search Tools : LinkedIn offers advanced job search tools that allow you to filter job postings by industry, location, and other criteria. Setting job alerts and following companies of interest can streamline your job search process.

5. Professional Development : LinkedIn Learning offers a wide range of courses on various topics. Investing time in these courses can help you acquire new skills and stay competitive in your industry.

Real-World Impact : Success Stories

LinkedIn's impact is best illustrated through real-world success stories. Here are a few examples :

1. John's Career Pivot : John, a mid-career professional in finance, was looking to transition into a data science role. He optimized his LinkedIn profile to highlight his analytical skills and completed relevant LinkedIn Learning courses. By engaging with data science communities on LinkedIn, he connected with a recruiter who eventually helped him land a data analyst position.

2. Sarah's Entrepreneurial Journey : Sarah, an entrepreneur, used LinkedIn to grow her business. By regularly sharing insights and articles about her industry, she positioned herself as a thought leader. Her active presence on LinkedIn helped her attract clients and partners, significantly expanding her business reach.

3. Mark's Job Search : Mark, a recent graduate, leveraged LinkedIn's job search tools to find his first job. By optimizing his profile, connecting with alumni, and actively applying to job postings, he secured a role at a top tech company within a few months of graduation.

LinkedIn for Businesses

LinkedIn is not just for individuals; it is a powerful tool for businesses as well. Here's how businesses can benefit from LinkedIn:

1. Brand Building : Companies can use LinkedIn to build and promote their brand. A well-crafted LinkedIn company page can showcase the company's values, culture, and achievements.

2. Recruitment : LinkedIn is a valuable resource for finding top talent. Companies can post job openings, search for candidates, and use LinkedIn's recruitment tools to streamline the hiring process.

3. Networking and Partnerships : LinkedIn facilitates B2B networking and partnerships. Companies can connect with potential partners, suppliers, and clients to explore new business opportunities.

4. Marketing and Sales : LinkedIn is an effective platform for marketing and sales. Through targeted advertising, content marketing, and lead generation tools, companies can reach their target audience and drive sales.

LinkedIn's Unique Features

Several unique features make LinkedIn a powerful platform :

1. Endorsements and Recommendations : These features allow peers to vouch for your skills and experiences, adding credibility to your profile.

2. Groups : LinkedIn Groups provide a space for professionals with similar interests to share ideas, seek advice, and collaborate.

3. Publishing Platform : LinkedIn's publishing platform allows users to share long-form content, such as articles and blogs, establishing themselves as thought leaders.

4. LinkedIn Learning : This feature offers a vast library of courses on various topics, helping users to continuously improve their skills.

The Future of LinkedIn

As LinkedIn continues to evolve, its importance in the professional world is only set to increase. The platform is constantly adding new features and tools to enhance user experience and provide more value. Here are some trends to watch :

1. AI and Personalization : LinkedIn is increasingly using artificial intelligence to provide personalized content, job recommendations, and connection suggestions.

2. Remote Work and Virtual Networking : The rise of remote work has made virtual networking more important than ever. LinkedIn is likely to continue developing tools to support virtual collaboration and networking.

3. Enhanced Analytics : LinkedIn is enhancing its analytics tools to help users better understand their profile performance and engagement.

4. Focus on Learning and Development : With the growing importance of continuous learning, LinkedIn Learning is expected to expand its offerings and become an even more integral part of the platform.

The Benefits of an Optimized Profile

In the digital era, your LinkedIn profile is often the first impression you make on potential employers, clients, and business partners. An optimized LinkedIn profile serves as a powerful tool to enhance your professional image and open doors to a multitude of opportunities.

Here are the key benefits of having an optimized LinkedIn profile :

1. Enhanced Visibility : An optimized profile increases your visibility on LinkedIn. By incorporating relevant keywords and maintaining an active presence, you improve your chances of appearing in search results conducted by recruiters, potential clients, and industry peers.

2. Professional Branding : Your LinkedIn profile is a reflection of your personal brand. A well-crafted profile allows you to showcase your unique skills, experiences, and accomplishments. It communicates your professional identity and sets you apart from others in your field.

3. Networking Opportunities : LinkedIn is a vast network of professionals from various industries. An optimized profile helps you connect with key individuals who can influence your career, including colleagues, industry leaders, mentors, and potential collaborators.

4. Job Opportunities : Many recruiters and hiring managers use LinkedIn as a primary tool to find and vet candidates. An optimized profile increases your chances of being discovered by recruiters and being considered for job opportunities that match your skills and career aspirations.

5. Credibility and Trust : Features like endorsements and recommendations add credibility to your profile. When others vouch for your skills and expertise, it builds trust and confidence among your network and potential employers.

6. Industry Insights and Learning : By following industry leaders and participating in LinkedIn groups, you gain access to valuable insights and discussions. This continuous learning helps you stay updated with industry trends and enhances your professional growth.

7. Showcasing Achievements : Your LinkedIn profile is an excellent platform to highlight your professional achievements. Whether it's a project you led, an award you received, or a milestone you achieved, showcasing these accomplishments reinforces your expertise and professional value.

8. Business Growth : For entrepreneurs and business owners, LinkedIn provides opportunities to promote your business, connect with potential clients, and build partnerships. An optimized company page can attract interest and generate leads for your business.

9. Engagement with Content : Sharing and engaging with content on LinkedIn positions you as a thought leader in your industry. Regularly posting updates, articles, and comments helps you stay relevant and visible within your professional community.

10. Access to LinkedIn Learning : An optimized profile often includes a commitment to ongoing learning. LinkedIn Learning offers a plethora of courses that can enhance your skills and knowledge, making you more competitive in the job market.

What to Expect from This Book

This book is designed to be a comprehensive guide to optimizing your LinkedIn profile, tailored to meet the needs of professionals across various industries. Here's what you can expect to learn :

1. Step-by-Step Guidance : Each chapter provides detailed, step-by-step instructions on how to optimize different sections of your LinkedIn profile, from crafting a compelling headline to writing an engaging summary and detailing your work experience.

2. Practical Examples : We include numerous examples and case studies of successful LinkedIn profiles from key personalities and businesses. These examples serve as inspiration and provide practical insights into what makes a profile stand out.

3. Industry-Specific Tips : The book offers tailored advice for professionals in different industries, helping you highlight the skills and experiences most relevant to your field. Whether you're in technology, finance, healthcare, or any other sector, you'll find tips to make your profile shine.

4. Networking Strategies : Learn effective strategies for building and maintaining a strong professional network on LinkedIn. We cover how to connect with others, engage with your network, and leverage connections for career growth.

5. Job Search Techniques : For job seekers, the book provides in-depth strategies on how to use LinkedIn's job search tools effectively. You'll learn how to optimize your profile for recruiters, set up job alerts, and apply to positions that match your skills.

6. Content Creation and Engagement : Discover the power of content on LinkedIn. We guide you on how to create and share valuable content, engage with others' posts, and establish yourself as a thought leader in your industry.

7. Using LinkedIn Analytics : Understand how to use LinkedIn's analytics tools to track the performance of your profile and content. Learn how to interpret data and make informed decisions to improve your LinkedIn presence.

8. Advanced Features : Explore LinkedIn's advanced features, such as LinkedIn Learning, endorsements, recommendations, and advertising. We provide tips on how to leverage these features to enhance your profile and achieve your professional goals.

9. Ongoing Maintenance : An optimized LinkedIn profile requires regular updates and engagement. The book offers advice on how to keep your profile current, engage with your network consistently, and monitor your progress.

10. Real-World Success Stories : Throughout the book, you'll find success stories and case studies of individuals and businesses who have effectively used LinkedIn to advance their careers and achieve their goals. These stories provide valuable lessons and inspiration.

By the end of this book, you will have the knowledge and tools to create a standout LinkedIn profile, build a robust professional network, and leverage LinkedIn's features to enhance your career or business. Whether you're a seasoned professional, a job seeker, or an entrepreneur, this guide will help you make the most of LinkedIn's vast potential.

Absolutely! Let's dive into Chapter 1 and cover the essentials of getting started with LinkedIn.

Chapter 1

GETTING STARTED WITH LINKEDIN

Creating an Account

Before you can take advantage of LinkedIn's vast network and powerful features, you need to create an account. This section will guide you through the process, ensuring you start with a strong foundation.

Step-by-Step Guide to Creating an Account

1. Visit the LinkedIn Website or Download the App : Start by visiting [LinkedIn's website](https : //www.linkedin.com) or downloading the LinkedIn app from your device's app store.

2. **Sign Up :** On the homepage, you'll see an option to sign up. Click on "Join now" if you're using the website or tap "Sign up" on the app.

3. **Enter Your Information :** You'll need to provide basic information, including your first name, last name, email address, and a password. Use a professional email address if possible, as this will be associated with your professional brand.

4. Location Details : LinkedIn will ask for your country and postal code to better connect you with relevant local opportunities and networks.

5. Job Title and Company : Enter your current job title and company. If you're a student, select the "I'm a student" option and provide your school details.

6. Verification : LinkedIn may ask you to verify your email address. Check your email for a verification link and follow the instructions to confirm your account.

7. Profile Picture : Upload a professional photo. Profiles with photos receive significantly more views. Choose a clear, high-resolution image where you are dressed appropriately for your industry.

8. Add Your Contacts : LinkedIn will prompt you to add contacts by syncing with your email address book. This step is optional, but it can help you start building your network quickly.

9. Customize Your Profile URL : LinkedIn assigns a default URL to your profile, which you can customize to make it more memorable. For example, you can change it to linkedin.com/in/YourName.

10. Complete Your Profile : LinkedIn will guide you through additional steps to complete your profile, such as adding your education, skills, and a summary.

Congratulations! You've created your LinkedIn account. Now let's explore the platform and understand its key features.

Understanding LinkedIn

LinkedIn is more than just an online resume. It's a dynamic platform designed for professional networking, job searching, learning, and content sharing. Here's an overview of LinkedIn's key features and how you can use them to your advantage.

The LinkedIn Home Page

The home page is your dashboard for all LinkedIn activities. Here's what you'll find :

1. News Feed : The center of your home page is the news feed, where you'll see updates from your connections, companies you follow, and content relevant to your interests. Engaging with posts by liking, commenting, and sharing helps you stay visible in your network.

2. Search Bar : At the top of the page, the search bar allows you to find people, jobs, companies, groups, and content. Use keywords and filters to refine your search results.

3. Notifications : The bell icon alerts you to notifications, such as connection requests, messages, and updates from your network. Regularly check your notifications to stay informed and responsive.

4. Messaging : The messaging icon lets you send and receive messages from your connections. LinkedIn messages are a great way to network, follow up on connections, and stay in touch with your professional contacts.

5. Profile : Clicking on your profile picture or name takes you to your profile page, where you can view and edit your details. This is your personal brand space on LinkedIn.

Key Features of LinkedIn

1. Profile : Your profile is the heart of your LinkedIn presence. It includes your photo, headline, summary, work experience, education, skills, endorsements, recommendations, and more. A complete and polished profile attracts more views and opportunities.

2. My Network : This section helps you manage your connections. Here, you can see invitations, people you may know, and your current connections. Building and maintaining your network is crucial for leveraging LinkedIn's full potential.

3. Jobs : The jobs section is a powerful tool for job seekers. You can search for jobs, save job postings, set up job alerts, and see how you're connected to hiring companies. LinkedIn also provides job recommendations based on your profile.

4. Notifications : This feature keeps you updated on activities in your network, such as connection requests, likes, comments, and mentions. Staying active and responsive to notifications helps maintain your professional presence.

5. Messaging : LinkedIn's messaging system allows you to communicate privately with your connections. You can also use InMail (a premium feature) to message people you're not connected with.

6. LinkedIn Learning : This feature offers a vast library of online courses on various topics. Investing time in LinkedIn Learning can help you acquire new skills and stay competitive.

7. Groups : LinkedIn groups are communities of professionals with shared interests. Joining groups relevant to your industry or interests can help you network, share knowledge, and stay updated on trends.

8. Events : LinkedIn allows you to create and attend professional events. Participating in events is a great way to network and learn from industry experts.

9. Company Pages : Follow companies you're interested in to get updates on their activities, job postings, and industry news. Company pages also provide insights into the company's culture and values.

10. Content Sharing : Sharing content on LinkedIn, such as articles, posts, and videos, can help you establish yourself as a thought leader. Engaging with others' content also enhances your visibility and professional relationships.

Navigating LinkedIn

Getting familiar with LinkedIn's interface and features is essential to make the most of the platform. Here are some tips to help you navigate LinkedIn effectively :

1. Regularly Update Your Profile : Keep your profile information current. Update your job title, work experience, skills, and profile picture as needed.

2. Engage with Your Network : Like, comment, and share posts from your connections. Engaging with content helps you stay visible and strengthens your relationships.

3. Expand Your Network : Actively seek out and connect with professionals in your industry. Personalized connection requests are more likely to be accepted.

4. Utilize Advanced Search : Use LinkedIn's advanced search filters to find people, jobs, and companies that match your criteria.

5. Take Advantage of LinkedIn Learning : Continuously develop your skills by enrolling in courses relevant to your career goals.

6. Join Groups : Participate in LinkedIn groups to expand your network, gain insights, and contribute to discussions.

7. Follow Companies and Influencers : Stay informed about industry trends and job opportunities by following relevant companies and thought leaders.

8. Monitor Your Analytics : Use LinkedIn's analytics tools to track your profile views, post engagement, and network growth. Analyzing this data can help you improve your LinkedIn strategy.

By understanding and utilizing these features, you can fully leverage LinkedIn to advance your career, build your network, and achieve your professional goals. The next chapters of this book will delve deeper into specific strategies and tips to optimize your LinkedIn profile and make the most of this powerful platform.

Chapter 2

CRAFTING A COMPELLING HEADLINE

The Power of the Headline

Your LinkedIn headline is one of the most critical elements of your profile. It's the first piece of information people see after your name, and it significantly influences whether they'll click on your profile to learn more. A compelling headline can set you apart from millions of other professionals on the platform. Here's why your headline matters and how you can make it powerful :

Why the Headline is Crucial

1. First Impressions : Your headline is often the first impression you make on LinkedIn. A well-crafted headline can capture attention, convey your professional identity, and entice viewers to read further.

2. Searchability : LinkedIn's search algorithms heavily rely on keywords. Including relevant keywords in your headline increases your chances of appearing in search results when recruiters or potential clients look for professionals with your skills and experience.

3. Professional Branding : Your headline is an opportunity to define your personal brand succinctly. It communicates who you are, what you do, and what makes you unique in just a few words.

4. Engagement : A compelling headline can boost engagement with your profile. More views and connections can lead to more opportunities, whether you're job hunting, seeking clients, or looking to network.

Key Elements of a Powerful Headline

1. Clarity : Your headline should clearly convey what you do. Avoid jargon or complex terms that might confuse viewers.

2. Keywords : Include keywords related to your industry, skills, and job role. Think about what terms potential employers or clients might search for.

3. Value Proposition : Highlight what you bring to the table. What value do you offer? This could be a specific skill set, unique expertise, or a proven track record of success.

4. Specificity : Be specific about your role and industry. Instead of a generic title like "Consultant," specify your niche, such as "Marketing Consultant Specializing in Digital Strategies for Tech Startups."

5. Personality : Inject a bit of your personality into your headline. This can make you more relatable and memorable. However, ensure it remains professional and appropriate for your industry.

Examples of Effective Headlines

To inspire you, here are some examples of effective LinkedIn headlines across various industries :

1. Technology Sector

- "Software Engineer | Full Stack Developer | Specializing in

JavaScript and Python"

- "Tech Lead | AI Enthusiast | Driving Innovation in Machine Learning Solutions"

2. Marketing and Sales

- "Digital Marketing Strategist | Helping Brands Grow through Data-Driven Campaigns"

- "Sales Director | Expert in SaaS Solutions | Passionate about Customer Success"

3. Healthcare

- "Registered Nurse | Pediatric Care Specialist | Advocating for Child Health and Wellness"

- "Healthcare Administrator | Streamlining Operations | Improving Patient Outcomes"

4. Finance

- "Certified Financial Planner | Helping Individuals Achieve Financial Independence"

- "Investment Analyst | Focused on Sustainable and Ethical Investments"

5. Education

- "High School Teacher | STEM Educator | Inspiring the Next Generation of Innovators"

- "University Professor | Researcher in Environmental Science | Published Author"

6. Entrepreneurship

- "Founder & CEO | Empowering Small Businesses with Digital Tools"

- "Serial Entrepreneur | Passionate about Startups and Innovation"

7. Creative Industries

- "Graphic Designer | Visual Storyteller | Expert in Branding and

Identity"

- "Content Writer | Crafting Engaging Stories | Specializing in Tech and Finance"

These examples showcase clarity, relevant keywords, value propositions, and a touch of personality, making them effective in grabbing attention and conveying professional value.

Creating Your Own Headline

Now that you understand the importance and elements of a compelling headline, it's time to create your own. Follow these steps to craft a headline that stands out :

Step-by-Step Guide

1. Identify Your Core Role and Skills : Start by listing your primary job role and key skills. What are the most important aspects of your professional identity?

2. Incorporate Keywords : Think about the keywords relevant to your industry and role. These should be terms that recruiters or potential clients might use to search for professionals like you.

3. Highlight Your Value Proposition : What value do you offer? This could be a specific expertise, a unique approach, or a significant achievement. Make sure this is clear in your headline.

4. Be Specific and Concise : Avoid vague terms and generalities. Be specific about your role, skills, and industry. Keep your headline concise, ideally under 120 characters, to ensure it's fully visible.

5. Add a Personal Touch : If appropriate, add a touch of your personality to make your headline more engaging. This could be a passion, a unique aspect of your work, or a professional mantra.

6. Review and Refine : Review your headline to ensure it's clear, impactful, and free of jargon. Ask for feedback from colleagues or mentors to refine it further.

Template and Examples

Here's a template you can use to structure your headline :

[Job Title] | [Key Skill/Expertise] | [Value Proposition/Unique Selling Point]

Examples :

- "Project Manager | Agile and Scrum Specialist | Delivering Projects On-Time and Within Budget"

- "UX/UI Designer | Enhancing User Experience | Creating Intuitive Digital Interfaces"

- "Public Relations Expert | Media Relations and Crisis Management | Building Brand Reputation"

Final Checklist

Before finalizing your headline, run through this checklist to ensure it's optimized :

- Is it clear and specific?
- Does it include relevant keywords?
- Does it highlight your value proposition?
- Is it concise and free of jargon?
- Does it reflect your professional identity and personality?

Leveraging ChatGPT to Write a Compelling Headline

Using AI tools like ChatGPT can help you craft a compelling LinkedIn headline. By providing the right prompts, you can get creative and effective suggestions tailored to your needs. Here's how you can leverage ChatGPT :

Effective Prompts for ChatGPT

To get the best results, use clear and specific prompts. Here are some examples :

1. Basic Professional Role :

- "I am a software engineer with 5 years of experience in full stack development. Suggest a LinkedIn headline."

- "I am a digital marketing strategist who specializes in social media campaigns for non-profits. Create a compelling LinkedIn headline for me."

2. Highlighting Key Skills :

- "I am a project manager skilled in Agile and Scrum methodologies. What should my LinkedIn headline be?"

- "I am a UX designer with expertise in user research and prototyping. Provide a LinkedIn headline that reflects this."

3. Including Value Proposition :

- "I help small businesses grow their online presence through SEO and content marketing. Suggest a LinkedIn headline that captures this."

- "I am a financial analyst focused on sustainable investments. What would be a good LinkedIn headline?"

4. Combining Multiple Aspects :

- "I am a healthcare administrator with 10 years of experience, known for improving patient outcomes. Create a LinkedIn headline for me."

- "I am a graphic designer and visual storyteller who excels in branding and identity. Provide a LinkedIn headline that includes these elements."

Sample Outputs-

Here are some sample outputs you might receive from ChatGPT based on the prompts above :

1. For a Software Engineer :

- "Software Engineer | Expert in Full Stack Development | Creating Scalable Web Solutions"

2. For a Digital Marketing Strategist :

- "Digital Marketing Strategist | Social Media Campaigns for Non-Profits | Driving Engagement and Awareness"

3. For a Project Manager :

- "Project Manager | Agile and Scrum Specialist | Delivering Projects On-Time and Within Budget"

4. For a UX Designer :

- "UX Designer | Expert in User Research and Prototyping | Crafting Intuitive Digital Experiences"

5. For an SEO and Content Marketing Specialist :

- "SEO and Content Marketing Expert | Boosting Small Business Online Presence | Driving Organic Growth"

6. For a Financial Analyst :

- "Financial Analyst | Specializing in Sustainable Investments | Driving Ethical Financial Growth"

7. For a Healthcare Administrator :

- "Healthcare Administrator | 10 Years of Experience | Enhancing Patient Outcomes and Operational Efficiency"

8. For a Graphic Designer :

- "Graphic Designer | Visual Storyteller | Expert in Branding and Identity" By leveraging ChatGPT, you can quickly generate creative and tailored headlines that effectively showcase your professional brand and value proposition.

Chapter 3

WRITING AN ENGAGING SUMMARY

What Makes a Great Summary : Key Elements to Include

Your LinkedIn summary, also known as the "About" section, is your chance to tell your professional story in a compelling way. It's where you can showcase your personality, highlight your achievements, and provide a narrative that goes beyond the bullet points of your resume. A well-crafted summary can captivate readers, making them want to learn more about you and engage with you. This section will delve into what makes a great summary and the key elements you should include to make yours stand out.

The Importance of a Great Summary

The LinkedIn summary is a critical component of your profile. Here's why it matters so much :

1. First Impressions : Your summary is one of the first sections people read after your headline. It sets the tone for the rest of your profile and can make or break the reader's interest in you.

2. Storytelling Opportunity : Unlike other sections of your profile, the summary allows for narrative and personality. It's where you can provide context to your career, explain your passions, and show what drives you.

3. SEO Benefits : A well-written summary with relevant keywords can improve your visibility in LinkedIn searches, making it easier for recruiters and potential clients to find you.

4. Engagement : An engaging summary encourages readers to connect with you, follow you, or even reach out with opportunities.

Key Elements of a Great Summary

To write an engaging summary, you need to include several key elements. Each element plays a unique role in conveying your professional identity and value. Here's a detailed breakdown of these elements :

1. Compelling Opening
2. Professional Overview
3. Key Achievements and Skills
4. Personal Touch
5. Call to Action
6. SEO and Keywords

1. Compelling Opening

Your opening lines are crucial for grabbing attention. Here's how to craft an engaging opening :

Why It Matters : The first few sentences of your summary should hook the reader, enticing them to read further. A strong opening differentiates you from others and sets the stage for your story.

How to Do It :

- Start with a Bold Statement or Question : A thought-provoking question or a bold statement can pique curiosity. For example, "What drives someone to leave a successful corporate career and start from scratch?"

- Highlight a Unique Achievement or Experience : Begin with an accomplishment or an experience that's significant and unique to you. "From leading a $10 million project to being recognized as the youngest CMO in my company's history…"

- Share a Personal Anecdote : A brief, relevant personal story can humanize you and draw readers in. "Ever since I sold my first lemonade at the age of 7, I knew I was destined for a career in business."

Examples :

- "Imagine transforming a struggling startup into a market leader within three years – that's my story."

- "Passionate about tech, I coded my first software program at age 12. Today, I lead a team of innovative developers at XYZ Corp."

2. Professional Overview

This section provides a snapshot of your career journey, highlighting your roles, industries, and the impact you've made.

Why It Matters : A clear professional overview helps readers quickly understand your background, expertise, and career trajectory. It establishes credibility and context.

How to Do It :

- Summarize Your Career Path : Provide a brief overview of your career, mentioning key roles and industries. "With over 15 years in the finance sector, I've held roles ranging from analyst to CFO."

- Highlight Major Responsibilities : Focus on responsibilities that demonstrate your skills and leadership. "I specialize in strategic planning, financial analysis, and team leadership."

- Emphasize Your Impact : Mention the impact you've had in your roles, using specific metrics if possible. "I've successfully led projects that increased revenue by 30% and improved operational efficiency by 25%."

Examples :

- "With a decade of experience in digital marketing, I have developed and executed strategies that have boosted online engagement by over 200% for top-tier brands."

- "As a project manager in the construction industry, I've overseen the completion of multimillion-dollar projects, ensuring they were delivered on time and within budget."

3. Key Achievements and Skills

Detailing your achievements and skills showcases your capabilities and sets you apart from others in your field.

Why It Matters : This section highlights your expertise and accomplishments, demonstrating the value you bring to potential employers, clients, or collaborators.

How to Do It :

- Highlight Major Achievements : Mention specific accomplishments, using numbers to quantify your success. "Increased sales by 40% in Q1 2023 through innovative marketing campaigns."

- Detail Relevant Skills : List key skills that are relevant to your industry and role. "Expert in Python, JavaScript, and cloud computing."

- Showcase Certifications and Awards : Include any certifications, awards, or recognitions that add to your credibility. "Certified Project Management Professional (PMP) and recipient of the 2021 Innovation Award."

Examples :

- "Awarded 'Top Salesperson of the Year' for three consecutive years by consistently exceeding sales targets by 20%."

- "Certified Data Analyst with expertise in machine learning, predictive analytics, and data visualization."

4. Personal Touch

Adding a personal touch to your summary helps readers relate to you on a human level, making you more memorable.

Why It Matters : Humanizing your profile can make you more approachable and relatable, fostering a sense of connection and trust with the reader.

How to Do It :

- **Share Personal Interests :** Mention hobbies or interests that reflect your personality. "Avid mountain biker and photography enthusiast."

- **Discuss Your Values and Passions :** Highlight what you're passionate about and what drives you. "Passionate about environmental sustainability and committed to green technology initiatives."

- **Include Volunteer Work :** If you're involved in any volunteer work or community service, mention it here. "Active volunteer with Habitat for Humanity, helping build homes for those in need."

Examples :

- "Outside of work, I'm an enthusiastic traveler who has explored over 20 countries, always seeking new cultures and experiences."

- "I'm passionate about mentoring young professionals and regularly participate in local tech meetups to share my knowledge and learn from others."

5. Call to Action

Conclude your summary with a clear call to action, encouraging readers to connect with you or learn more about your work.

Why It Matters : A call to action guides the reader on what to do next, whether it's connecting with you, visiting your website, or reaching out for collaboration.

How to Do It :

- Invite Connections : Encourage readers to connect with you. "Feel free to connect with me to discuss how we can collaborate."

- Offer Further Engagement : Suggest ways they can learn more about you or your work. "Visit my portfolio at [website] to see my latest projects."

- Express Availability : Mention your openness to opportunities. "Currently open to new opportunities in digital marketing and project management."

Examples :

- "Let's connect to explore how we can drive innovation together. Reach out to me at [email] or through LinkedIn messaging."

- "Check out my recent projects at [website] and let's discuss how we can collaborate on future endeavors."

6. SEO and Keywords

Incorporating relevant keywords into your summary can improve your profile's visibility in search results.

Why It Matters : Keywords help LinkedIn's search algorithm understand your profile's relevance to specific searches, increasing the chances that recruiters or potential clients will find you.

How to Do It :

- Identify Relevant Keywords : Think about the terms that are most relevant to your industry, role, and skills. Use LinkedIn's search feature to see what keywords other professionals in your field are using.

- **Integrate Keywords Naturally :** Incorporate these keywords seamlessly into your summary. Avoid keyword stuffing; instead, ensure they fit naturally within your narrative.

- **Use Variations of Keywords :** Include different variations of key terms to cover all bases. For instance, use both "project management" and "project manager."

Examples :

- "As a digital marketing specialist, I excel in SEO, content marketing, and social media strategy. My expertise in Google Analytics and PPC campaigns has driven significant growth for my clients."

- "With over 15 years of experience as a software engineer, I am proficient in Java, Python, and cloud computing. My work in developing scalable web applications has been recognized industry-wide."

Crafting Your Summary : A Step-by-Step Guide

Now that we've outlined the key elements of a great summary, let's go through the process of crafting your own, step by step.

1. Draft Your Opening Lines : Start with a hook that grabs attention. Write a bold statement, share a personal anecdote, or highlight a unique achievement.

2. Write Your Professional Overview : Summarize your career path, including key roles and industries. Highlight major responsibilities and the impact you've made.

3. List Your Key Achievements and Skills : Detail your major accomplishments and relevant skills. Include any certifications or awards that add to your credibility.

4. Add a Personal Touch : Share your interests, values, and any volunteer work. This humanizes your profile and makes you more relatable.

5. Include a Call to Action : Conclude with a clear call to action, encouraging readers to connect with you or learn more about your work.

6. Incorporate Keywords : Identify relevant keywords and integrate them naturally into your summary. Ensure they fit seamlessly within your narrative.

7. Review and Refine : Read through your summary several times. Ensure it flows well, is free of jargon, and effectively communicates your professional story. Ask for feedback from trusted colleagues or mentors to refine it further.

Examples of Great LinkedIn Summaries

To give you a clearer picture, here are some examples of great LinkedIn summaries that incorporate all the key elements :

Example 1 : Marketing Professional

"As a digital marketing strategist with over a decade of experience, I specialize in crafting data-driven campaigns that drive engagement and conversion. My journey began at ABC Corp, where I spearheaded initiatives that boosted online engagement by over 200%. Today, I lead a dynamic team at XYZ Marketing, where we help brands navigate the complexities of the digital landscape. Passionate about storytelling and consumer psychology, I blend creativity with analytics to deliver compelling marketing solutions. My expertise spans SEO, content marketing, social media strategy, and Google Analytics. Recognized as 'Marketer of the Year' by the DMA, I thrive on creating impactful campaigns that resonate with audiences. Outside the office, I'm an avid traveler who finds inspiration in exploring new cultures. I'm also committed to giving back, volunteering with local non-profits to help them amplify their message through digital channels. Let's connect and explore how we can create marketing magic together. Reach out to me at [email] or through LinkedIn messaging.``

Example 2 : Software Engineer

"Imagine developing software that powers millions of devices around the world – that's the journey I'm on as a software engineer. With over 15 years of experience in full stack development, I've honed my skills in Java, Python, and cloud computing. At Tech Innovators Inc., I lead a team dedicated to creating scalable, high-performance applications. My career highlights include leading the development of a cloud-based platform that increased user engagement by 30%, and implementing a machine learning algorithm that improved data processing speeds by 50%. Certified in AWS and recognized as a thought leader in software architecture, I'm passionate about leveraging technology to solve complex problems.

Beyond coding, I'm a mountain biking enthusiast and a lifelong learner, constantly exploring new technologies and methodologies. Actively involved in mentoring junior developers, I believe in the power of collaboration and continuous improvement. Interested in discussing innovative software solutions or just sharing tech insights? Connect with me here on LinkedIn."

Example 3 : Financial Analyst

"With a passion for numbers and a knack for strategic thinking, I've built a career as a financial analyst dedicated to driving sustainable financial growth. Over the past 10 years, I've worked with leading firms like XYZ Finance, where I developed financial models that informed key business decisions and optimized investment portfolios.

My expertise lies in financial planning, data analysis, and sustainable investments. I'm particularly proud of my role in transitioning our firm's portfolio to include 50% more eco-friendly investments, which not only boosted returns but also aligned with our commitment to ethical finance. As a CFA charterholder, I stay ahead of market trends and regulatory changes. Outside of work, I'm an advocate for financial literacy and volunteer with organizations that teach budgeting and investment basics to underserved communities. I'm also an avid reader and a hiking enthusiast. Let's connect to discuss financial strategies or share insights on sustainable investing. Reach out to me via LinkedIn messaging or at [email]."

Personal Branding : How to Present Your Personal Brand Effectively

Personal branding is about crafting and projecting a professional identity that distinguishes you from others in your field. Your LinkedIn summary is a prime canvas for this, allowing you to present your unique value proposition and professional persona in a compelling narrative. Here's how to present your personal brand effectively in your LinkedIn summary :

Why Personal Branding Matters

1. Differentiation : In a crowded marketplace, a strong personal brand helps you stand out. It communicates what makes you unique and why someone should connect with you or hire you over someone else.

2. **Consistency :** A well-defined personal brand ensures consistency across your professional communications and online presence. This consistency builds trust and recognition.

3. Reputation : Your personal brand shapes how others perceive you. A positive, well-crafted brand can enhance your reputation and open up new opportunities.

Steps to Present Your Personal Brand

1. Define Your Unique Value Proposition (UVP) : Your UVP is the core of your personal brand. It's a clear statement that explains what you do, how you do it differently, and the value you bring to your clients or employer.

- Ask Yourself : What are your key skills? What makes your approach unique? What achievements set you apart?

- Example : "As a data scientist, I transform complex data into actionable insights, helping companies make data-driven decisions that drive growth."

2. Craft Your Personal Story : People connect with stories. Your summary should tell the story of your professional journey, highlighting key experiences and achievements that define your career path.

- Start with a Hook : Grab attention with an intriguing fact or a bold statement.

- Narrate Your Journey : Use a narrative style to walk the reader through your career highlights.

- Example : "From analyzing weather patterns as a meteorology student to optimizing logistics for Fortune 500 companies, my journey as a data analyst has always been about uncovering hidden patterns and driving efficiency."

3. Highlight Key Achievements and Skills : Showcase your most significant accomplishments and skills, quantifying them where possible to add impact.

- Be Specific : Use numbers and specific examples to demonstrate your expertise.

- Example : "Increased organic traffic by 150% in six months through targeted SEO strategies."

4. Show Your Personality and Values : Infuse your summary with elements of your personality and professional values. This makes you more relatable and memorable.

- Share Personal Interests : Briefly mention hobbies or interests that reflect your personality.

- Example : "When I'm not crafting marketing strategies, you'll find me exploring nature trails or volunteering at the local animal shelter."

5. Include a Call to Action : Encourage readers to take the next step, whether it's connecting with you, visiting your website, or reaching out for collaboration.

- Be Clear and Direct : End with a clear invitation to connect or learn more about you.

- Example : "Let's connect and explore how we can collaborate to achieve your business goals. Feel free to reach out via LinkedIn messaging or email."

Examples and Templates : Sample Summaries from Different Industries

Crafting a compelling LinkedIn summary requires creativity and understanding of your industry. Here are sample summaries across various fields to inspire you.

Technology Sector

Software Engineer

"As a seasoned software engineer with over 10 years of experience in full-stack development, I specialize in building scalable web applications that solve real-world problems. My expertise spans

JavaScript, Python, and cloud technologies, with a keen focus on delivering robust and user-friendly solutions. At XYZ Corp, I led the development of an e-commerce platform that increased sales by 40% and improved customer retention by 30%. When I'm not coding, I enjoy exploring new tech trends and contributing to open-source projects. Let's connect to discuss innovative tech solutions or collaborate on cutting-edge projects."

Data Scientist

"Transforming data into actionable insights is my passion. With a PhD in Data Science and 8 years of industry experience, I have helped organizations leverage data to drive strategic decisions and operational efficiency. At ABC Analytics, I developed predictive models that reduced customer churn by 20% and enhanced marketing ROI by 35%. Proficient in Python, R, and SQL, I thrive on solving complex problems and unlocking new opportunities through data. Outside of work, I enjoy teaching data science workshops and mentoring aspiring data scientists. Reach out to discuss data strategies or potential collaborations."

Marketing and Sales

Digital Marketing Manager

"Driven by a passion for digital innovation, I have over 7 years of experience in creating and executing comprehensive marketing strategies that drive growth and engagement. At XYZ Marketing, I spearheaded campaigns that increased lead generation by 50% and improved conversion rates by 25%. My skills include SEO, content marketing, social media strategy, and data analytics. I'm committed to staying ahead of digital trends and continuously optimizing performance to deliver exceptional results. Let's connect to explore how we can elevate your brand's digital presence."

Sales Director

"With a proven track record of exceeding sales targets and driving business growth, I bring over 15 years of sales leadership experience to the table. At ABC Solutions, I led a high-performing sales team that achieved a 30% increase in annual revenue and expanded our client base by 40%. My expertise lies in strategic planning, relationship building, and negotiating high-value deals. Passionate about mentoring and developing sales talent, I believe in a collaborative approach to achieving success. Interested in discussing sales strategies or exploring partnership opportunities? Let's connect."

Healthcare

Healthcare Administrator

"Dedicated to improving patient outcomes and operational efficiency, I have over 12 years of experience in healthcare administration. At XYZ Hospital, I implemented process improvements that reduced patient wait times by 30% and increased patient satisfaction scores by 20%. My skills include strategic planning, healthcare management, and regulatory compliance. I'm passionate about leveraging technology to enhance healthcare delivery and ensure quality care for all patients. Outside of work, I volunteer with healthcare nonprofits to support community health initiatives. Let's connect to discuss healthcare innovations and best practices."

Registered Nurse

"Compassionate and detail-oriented, I have 8 years of experience as a registered nurse, specializing in pediatric care. At ABC Children's Hospital, I provide high-quality care to young patients, ensuring their comfort and well-being. My expertise includes patient assessment, care planning, and family education. Recognized for my dedication and empathy, I strive to make a positive impact on my patients' lives every day. In my free time, I volunteer at local health clinics and participate in health education programs. Let's connect to share insights on pediatric healthcare or collaborate on community health projects."

Finance

Financial Analyst

"With a strong analytical mindset and a passion for financial markets, I have 10 years of experience in financial analysis and investment management. At XYZ Investments, I conduct in-depth market research and develop investment strategies that maximize returns while mitigating risks.

My skills include financial modeling, portfolio management, and data analysis. Committed to ethical and sustainable investing, I help clients achieve their financial goals responsibly. Outside of work, I'm an avid reader of financial literature and enjoy sharing insights on investment trends. Let's connect to discuss investment opportunities and strategies."

Certified Public Accountant (CPA)

"Detail-oriented and results-driven, I have over 15 years of experience as a certified public accountant, specializing in tax planning and compliance. At ABC Accounting, I help clients navigate complex tax regulations and optimize their financial performance. My expertise includes tax preparation, financial reporting, and audit management. Recognized for my accuracy and integrity, I'm dedicated to providing top-notch accounting services. In my free time, I volunteer with local nonprofits to support financial literacy initiatives. Let's connect to discuss tax strategies and accounting solutions."

Education

High School Teacher

"Passionate about inspiring the next generation, I have 10 years of experience as a high school teacher, specializing in STEM education. At XYZ High School, I create engaging and interactive lessons that make science and math accessible and exciting for students. My commitment to student success is reflected in my students' improved test scores and enthusiasm for learning. Beyond the classroom, I mentor students in science clubs and coordinate educational field trips. Let's connect to share teaching strategies and collaborate on educational projects."

University Professor

"With a deep commitment to academic excellence and research, I have over 20 years of experience as a university professor in environmental science. At ABC University, I teach courses on climate change and sustainable development, while conducting research on renewable energy solutions.

My work has been published in leading scientific journals and has contributed to policy recommendations at the national level. Dedicated to mentoring students, I guide them in research projects and career development. Let's connect to discuss environmental research and educational initiatives."

Leveraging ChatGPT in Writing an Engaging Summary

Using AI tools like ChatGPT can help you craft an engaging LinkedIn summary by providing creative suggestions and refining your ideas. Here's how to leverage ChatGPT to enhance your summary :

Why Use ChatGPT

1. Creativity : ChatGPT can generate creative and unique ideas that you might not have considered.

2. Efficiency : It saves time by quickly producing draft content that you can refine and personalize.

3. Clarity : ChatGPT can help clarify your thoughts and present them in a coherent, engaging manner.

Effective Prompts for ChatGPT

To get the best results, use clear and specific prompts. Here are some examples :

1. General Professional Overview

- "I am a project manager with 10 years of experience in the construction industry. Can you help me write an engaging LinkedIn summary?"

- "As a digital marketing strategist specializing in social media campaigns, I need a LinkedIn summary that highlights my skills and achievements."

2. Highlighting Key Skills and Achievements

- "I have increased sales by 30% and led a team of 20 sales professionals. Can you draft a LinkedIn summary that showcases these accomplishments?"

- "I am a software engineer proficient in Java and Python, with a focus on developing scalable web applications. Can you create a LinkedIn summary that highlights my expertise?"

3. Personalizing with Interests and Values

- "I'm a financial analyst who enjoys teaching financial literacy to underserved communities. Can you write a LinkedIn summary that includes this personal touch?"

- "I am a registered nurse passionate about pediatric care and volunteering at local clinics. Can you draft a LinkedIn summary that reflects my professional and personal interests?"

4. Crafting a Compelling Opening

- "Start my LinkedIn summary with a bold statement about my passion for digital marketing and data analytics."

- "Can you help me open my LinkedIn summary with a personal story about why I chose a career in software engineering?"

Sample Outputs from ChatGPT

1. For a Project Manager

"With over a decade of experience in the construction industry, I have successfully managed multimillion-dollar projects, ensuring they were delivered on time and within budget. My expertise lies in project planning, risk management, and team leadership. I thrive on turning complex challenges into successful outcomes, as demonstrated by my track record of increasing project efficiency by 25%. Outside of work, I'm passionate about sustainable building practices and volunteer with organizations promoting green construction. Let's connect to discuss innovative construction solutions and project management strategies."

2. For a Digital Marketing Strategist

"As a digital marketing strategist with a knack for social media campaigns, I've helped brands boost their online presence and engagement. My strategies have led to a 30% increase in leads and a 50% growth in social media followers for my clients. Proficient in SEO, content marketing, and data analytics, I combine creativity with data-driven insights to deliver impactful marketing solutions. Beyond the digital world, I enjoy exploring new trends in marketing and mentoring young professionals. Let's connect to explore how we can drive your brand's digital success."

3. For a Software Engineer

"Passionate about coding and problem-solving, I have over 8 years of experience as a software engineer. Specializing in Java and Python, I develop scalable web applications that enhance user experience and efficiency. At Tech Innovators Inc., I led the development of a platform that increased user engagement by 40% and optimized performance by 30%. When I'm not coding, I enjoy contributing to open-source projects and staying updated on the latest tech trends. Let's connect to discuss innovative software solutions and collaborative opportunities."

4. For a Financial Analyst

"With a strong foundation in financial analysis and a passion for ethical investing, I have dedicated the past 10 years to helping clients achieve their financial goals. At XYZ Investments, I developed strategies that increased portfolio returns by 20% while aligning with sustainable investment principles. My expertise includes financial modeling, market research, and risk assessment. Committed to financial literacy, I volunteer to teach budgeting and investing basics to underserved communities. Let's connect to discuss sustainable investment opportunities and financial strategies."

By leveraging ChatGPT, you can quickly generate creative and tailored summaries that effectively communicate your professional story and personal brand. Use these examples and prompts as a starting point to craft a LinkedIn summary that stands out and resonates with your audience.

Conclusion

A great LinkedIn summary is more than just a list of your achievements – it's a story that showcases your professional journey, highlights your skills, and reflects your personality. By incorporating a compelling opening, a clear professional overview, key achievements and skills, a personal touch, a call to action, and relevant keywords, you can create a summary that engages readers and sets you apart.

Take the time to craft a summary that truly represents who you are and what you offer. Regularly update it to reflect your latest achievements and skills. With a well-written summary, you'll enhance your professional brand, increase your visibility, and open the door to new opportunities.

Chapter 4

DETAILING YOUR WORK EXPERIENCE

Highlighting Achievements : How to Showcase Your Accomplishments

Your work experience section is one of the most crucial parts of your LinkedIn profile. It not only outlines your professional history but also demonstrates your ability to deliver results and add value to an organization. Highlighting your achievements effectively can make a significant difference in how potential employers, clients, and collaborators perceive you. In this section, we'll explore how to showcase your accomplishments in various industries, emphasizing their importance for job seekers.

The Importance of Highlighting Achievements

1. Demonstrating Value : Achievements show your potential value to future employers. They provide tangible evidence of what you can accomplish, making you a more attractive candidate.

2. Differentiation : In a competitive job market, achievements help differentiate you from other candidates with similar roles or experiences. They highlight your unique contributions and successes.

3. Building Credibility : Specific accomplishments build credibility and trust. They indicate that you have a proven track record of success and can deliver results.

4. Career Progression : Showcasing your achievements effectively demonstrates your career progression and growth, which is important for recruiters and hiring managers looking for upwardly mobile candidates.

How to Highlight Achievements

To effectively showcase your achievements, follow these guidelines:

1. Be Specific and Quantify Results : Use specific numbers, percentages, and other quantifiable data to highlight your accomplishments. This adds credibility and impact to your statements.

2. Focus on Impact : Emphasize the impact of your achievements on the organization or project. This shows that your contributions had significant, positive outcomes.

3. Use Action Verbs : Start each bullet point with strong action verbs to convey a sense of dynamism and proactivity. Examples include "led," "improved," "developed," "increased," and "achieved."

4. Tailor to Your Industry : Highlight achievements that are particularly relevant to your industry. This makes your profile more compelling to recruiters and hiring managers in your field.

Industry-Specific Examples

Technology Sector

Software Engineer

Why It Matters : In the technology sector, demonstrating your ability to solve complex problems and deliver high-quality software is crucial. Quantifiable achievements show your technical expertise and impact.

How to Highlight :

- Improved Performance : "Developed and optimized a new algorithm that improved processing speed by 30%, enhancing user experience and reducing server costs."

- Project Leadership : "Led a team of five developers in the successful completion of a $2 million software project, delivering ahead of schedule and under budget."

- Innovation : "Designed and implemented a new feature that increased user engagement by 20% within the first three months of release."

Marketing and Sales

Digital Marketing Manager

Why It Matters : In marketing, results are often measured by metrics such as engagement, conversion rates, and ROI. Highlighting these metrics showcases your ability to drive business growth and execute effective campaigns.

How to Highlight :

- Increased Engagement : "Launched a social media campaign that increased engagement by 150%, leading to a 25% growth in website traffic."

- ROI : "Managed a $500,000 annual marketing budget, achieving a 35% ROI through targeted digital advertising and content marketing strategies."

- Lead Generation : "Developed and executed email marketing campaigns that generated over 10,000 new leads in six months."

Sales Director

Why It Matters : For sales roles, demonstrating your ability to close deals, meet targets, and contribute to revenue growth is essential. Highlighting specific achievements in these areas can set you apart from other candidates.

How to Highlight :

- Revenue Growth : "Increased regional sales revenue by 40% year-over-year, becoming the top-performing sales director in the company."

- Team Performance : "Led a team of 20 sales representatives to exceed quarterly sales targets by an average of 15% over two years."

- Client Acquisition : "Secured contracts with five new Fortune 500 clients, contributing to a $5 million increase in annual revenue."

Healthcare

Registered Nurse

Why It Matters : In healthcare, the quality of patient care and the ability to handle complex medical situations are paramount. Highlighting achievements in these areas demonstrates your competence and dedication.

How to Highlight :

- Patient Outcomes : "Implemented a new patient care protocol that reduced hospital readmission rates by 15%."

- Efficiency : "Streamlined the medication administration process, resulting in a 20% reduction in errors and improved patient safety."

- Recognition : "Awarded 'Nurse of the Year' for exceptional patient care and dedication to the nursing profession."

Healthcare Administrator

Why It Matters : Healthcare administrators need to showcase their ability to manage operations, improve efficiency, and enhance patient satisfaction. Highlighting these achievements is crucial for demonstrating leadership and strategic impact.

How to Highlight :

- Operational Efficiency : "Introduced a new scheduling system that increased operational efficiency by 25%, reducing patient wait times."

- Cost Savings : "Negotiated supplier contracts that saved the hospital $500,000 annually without compromising quality."

- Patient Satisfaction : "Implemented a patient feedback system that improved overall patient satisfaction scores by 30%."

Finance

Financial Analyst

Why It Matters : In finance, analytical skills and the ability to make data-driven decisions are critical. Highlighting achievements that demonstrate your impact on financial performance and strategic planning is essential.

How to Highlight :

- Investment Performance : "Developed and managed a portfolio that outperformed the market by 15% annually over three years."

- Cost Reduction : "Identified and implemented cost-saving measures that reduced departmental expenses by 10%."

- Strategic Analysis : "Conducted a financial analysis that led to a successful $50 million acquisition, enhancing company growth prospects."

Certified Public Accountant (CPA)

Why It Matters : CPAs must demonstrate their ability to manage finances accurately and effectively, ensuring compliance and optimizing financial performance. Highlighting specific achievements in these areas is crucial.

How to Highlight :

- Compliance : "Successfully led the audit process for multiple clients, ensuring 100% compliance with regulatory standards."

- Tax Savings : "Implemented tax strategies that resulted in $1 million in savings for corporate clients over two years."

- Financial Reporting : "Streamlined financial reporting processes, reducing month-end close time by 40% and improving accuracy."

Education

High School Teacher

Why It Matters : Teachers need to demonstrate their impact on student learning and development. Highlighting achievements in improving student performance and engagement can showcase your effectiveness as an educator.

How to Highlight :

- Student Performance : "Increased student pass rates in STEM subjects by 20% through innovative teaching methods and personalized support."

- Engagement : "Developed a project-based learning curriculum that increased student engagement and participation by 30%."

- Recognition : "Received 'Teacher of the Year' award for outstanding contributions to student success and curriculum development."

University Professor

Why It Matters : University professors need to showcase their contributions to academia through research, teaching, and mentorship. Highlighting achievements in these areas can enhance your academic profile.

How to Highlight :

- Research : "Published over 20 peer-reviewed articles in top scientific journals, contributing to advancements in environmental science."

- Teaching : "Developed a new course on climate change that became the most enrolled elective in the department."

- Mentorship : "Mentored graduate students, with 90% of mentees successfully completing their dissertations and securing academic positions."

Crafting Your Achievement Statements : A Step-by-Step Guide

1. Identify Key Achievements : Review your career history and identify key achievements that had a significant impact on your organization or project. Focus on accomplishments that are quantifiable and relevant to your industry.

2. Quantify Results : Whenever possible, use numbers to quantify your achievements. This could be percentages, dollar amounts, time saved, or any other measurable impact.

3. Use Action Verbs : Start each achievement with a strong action verb to convey a sense of dynamism and proactivity.

4. Provide Context and Impact : Briefly describe the context of your achievement and the impact it had on the organization. This helps the reader understand the significance of your contribution.

5. Tailor to Your Industry : Highlight achievements that are particularly relevant to your industry, making your profile more compelling to recruiters and hiring managers in your field.

Examples of Achievement Statements

Software Engineer

- "Developed and optimized a new algorithm that improved processing speed by 30%, enhancing user experience and reducing server costs."

- "Led a team of five developers in the successful completion of a $2 million software project, delivering ahead of schedule and under budget."

Digital Marketing Manager

- "Launched a social media campaign that increased engagement by 150%, leading to a 25% growth in website traffic."

- "Managed a $500,000 annual marketing budget, achieving a 35% ROI through targeted digital advertising and content marketing strategies."

Registered Nurse

- "Implemented a new patient care protocol that reduced hospital readmission rates by 15%."

- "Streamlined the medication administration process, resulting in a 20% reduction in errors and improved patient safety."

Financial Analyst

- "Developed and managed a portfolio that outperformed the market by 15% annually over three years."

- "Identified and implemented cost-saving measures that reduced departmental expenses by 10%."

High School Teacher

- "Increased student pass rates in STEM subjects by 20% through innovative teaching methods and personalized support."

- "Developed a project-based learning curriculum that increased student engagement and participation by 30%."

By following these guidelines and examples, you can effectively showcase your achievements on LinkedIn, demonstrating your value and making a compelling case for why you should be considered for new opportunities.

Using Keywords : Importance of Keywords for Visibility and Searchability

In the digital age, where recruiters and hiring managers often rely on LinkedIn's search function to find potential candidates, incorporating keywords into your work experience section is crucial. Keywords help ensure that your profile appears in relevant search results, increasing your visibility and chances of being discovered by the right people. Here's how to use keywords effectively :

The Importance of Keywords

1. Increased Visibility : Keywords increase your chances of appearing in search results when recruiters look for candidates with specific skills or experiences.

2. Relevance : By using industry-specific keywords, you can align your profile with what employers are looking for, making you a more attractive candidate.

3. SEO Benefits : Search Engine Optimization (SEO) is not just for websites; it applies to LinkedIn profiles as well. Proper keyword usage can enhance your profile's SEO, making it easier for others to find you.

How to Identify Relevant Keywords

1. Job Descriptions : Look at job descriptions for positions similar to yours. Identify common terms and phrases that employers use.

2. Industry Trends : Stay updated on industry trends and terminology. Use terms that are current and widely recognized in your field.

3. Skills and Endorsements : Review the skills listed in your LinkedIn endorsements and add any relevant ones to your experience descriptions.

Incorporating Keywords Naturally

1. Role Titles : Use standard job titles that are recognized in your industry. Avoid creative titles that might not be picked up by search algorithms.

2. Responsibilities and Achievements : Describe your responsibilities and achievements using keywords. For example, instead of saying "improved sales," say "enhanced sales through strategic digital marketing campaigns."

3. Skills : Mention specific skills that are relevant to your roles. For example, if you're a software developer, include terms like "JavaScript," "Python," and "Agile methodologies."

Examples of Keyword Usage

Marketing Manager

- "Developed and executed digital marketing strategies that increased online engagement by 40% using SEO, content marketing, and social media management."

- "Managed a team of five marketing professionals to create PPC campaigns that resulted in a 30% increase in conversion rates."

Financial Analyst

- "Conducted comprehensive financial analysis using Excel and SQL, providing actionable insights that led to a 15% reduction in operational costs."

- "Developed and maintained financial models for forecasting and budgeting, ensuring accurate financial planning and analysis."

Structuring Your Experience : Best Practices for Formatting and Content

The structure and format of your work experience section can significantly impact how effectively your achievements and roles are communicated. A well-organized and clearly formatted section ensures that readers can quickly understand your career history and accomplishments. Here are the best practices for structuring your work experience :

Consistent Formatting

1. Chronological Order : List your work experience in reverse chronological order, starting with your most recent position. This makes it easy for readers to see your career progression.

2. Standard Sections : Each job entry should include the following:

- Job Title : Use a clear and recognizable job title.

- Company Name : Include the full name of the company.

- Dates of Employment : Provide the month and year for the start and end of each position.

- Location : Indicate the city and state (or country) of the job location.

Clear and Concise Descriptions

1. Responsibilities : Use bullet points to list your main responsibilities. Keep each point concise and focused on key tasks.

2. Achievements : Include a separate section for your achievements under each role. Use bullet points to highlight specific accomplishments, quantifying them where possible.

Focus on Action and Impact

1. Action Verbs : Start each bullet point with a strong action verb to convey a sense of proactivity and achievement (e.g., "Developed," "Led," "Implemented").

2. Quantifiable Results : Whenever possible, quantify your achievements with numbers or percentages to provide clear evidence of your impact.

Tailor Content to Your Audience

1. Relevance : Focus on responsibilities and achievements that are most relevant to the roles you are seeking. Tailor your descriptions to highlight experiences that align with your career goals.

2. Keywords : Ensure that relevant keywords are integrated naturally into your descriptions to improve searchability.

Example of a Well-Structured Experience Entry

Digital Marketing Manager, XYZ Corp

January 2018 – Present, New York, NY

- Developed and executed comprehensive digital marketing strategies that increased online engagement by 40%.

- Managed a team of five marketing professionals to create and implement PPC campaigns, resulting in a 30% increase in conversion rates.

- Conducted market research and data analysis using Google Analytics, driving informed decision-making and optimizing marketing efforts.

- Improved SEO rankings by implementing on-page and off-page SEO techniques, leading to a 25% growth in organic traffic.

Achievements :

- Awarded "Employee of the Year" in 2020 for outstanding performance and contributions to the marketing department.

- Successfully launched a rebranding campaign that increased brand awareness by 50% within six months.

Leveraging ChatGPT for Detailing Your Work Experience

Using AI tools like ChatGPT can significantly streamline the process of detailing your work experience. ChatGPT can help you generate creative and impactful descriptions, refine your language, and ensure that your experience is communicated effectively. Here's how to leverage ChatGPT for this purpose :

Why Use ChatGPT

1. Creativity : ChatGPT can provide fresh ideas and creative ways to describe your responsibilities and achievements.

2. Efficiency : It saves time by quickly generating draft content that you can refine and personalize.

3. Clarity and Precision : ChatGPT can help clarify your thoughts and present them in a concise and engaging manner.

Effective Prompts for ChatGPT

To get the best results, use clear and specific prompts. Here are some examples :

1. General Role Descriptions

- "I am a project manager in the construction industry. Can you help me write a LinkedIn description that highlights my responsibilities and achievements?"

- "I'm a software engineer with expertise in Java and Python. Create a detailed description of my role for LinkedIn."

2. Highlighting Specific Achievements

- "I led a marketing campaign that increased engagement by 30%. Can you write a LinkedIn summary that includes this achievement?"

- "I developed a financial model that saved the company $1 million. How should I detail this in my work experience section?"

3. Tailoring Content to Industry

- "I work in healthcare administration. How should I describe my role and achievements on LinkedIn?"

- "As a high school teacher, what's the best way to highlight my impact on student performance and engagement?"

Sample Outputs from ChatGPT

1. For a Project Manager in Construction

"Project Manager, ABC Construction*

March 2016 – Present, Los Angeles, CA

- Led multiple construction projects valued at over $10 million, ensuring timely completion and adherence to budget constraints.

- Coordinated with architects, engineers, and subcontractors to deliver high-quality projects, improving client satisfaction by 20%.

- Implemented a new project management software, streamlining processes and reducing project delays by 15%.

- Conducted regular site inspections and safety audits, maintaining a zero-incident record over three years.

Achievements :

- Recognized for exceptional leadership and project management skills, receiving the 'Best Project Manager' award in 2019."

2. For a Software Engineer

"Software Engineer, Tech Innovators Inc.*

June 2014 – Present, San Francisco, CA

- Developed and optimized scalable web applications using Java and Python, enhancing system performance by 35%.

- Collaborated with cross-functional teams to design and implement new features, increasing user engagement by 25%.

- Conducted code reviews and provided mentorship to junior developers, fostering a collaborative and high-performing team environment.

- Utilized Agile methodologies to manage project timelines and deliverables, achieving a 98% on-time delivery rate.

Achievements :

- Awarded 'Employee of the Month' for outstanding performance and contributions to the development team."

3. For a Healthcare Administrator

"Healthcare Administrator, XYZ Hospital*

January 2015 – Present, Chicago, IL

- Oversaw daily operations of a 200-bed hospital, ensuring compliance with healthcare regulations and standards.

- Implemented a new electronic health record (EHR) system, reducing patient wait times by 20% and improving overall efficiency.

- Developed and executed strategic plans to enhance patient care services, resulting in a 15% increase in patient satisfaction scores.

- Managed a team of healthcare professionals, providing training and support to improve staff performance and morale.

Achievements :

- Successfully negotiated contracts with suppliers, saving the hospital $500,000 annually."

4. For a High School Teacher

"High School Teacher, ABC High School*

September 2012 – Present, Boston, MA

- Designed and delivered engaging STEM curricula that improved student pass rates by 20%.

- Implemented project-based learning strategies, increasing student participation and enthusiasm for STEM subjects.

- Organized and led extracurricular science clubs and field trips, enhancing students' practical knowledge and interest in science.

- Provided personalized support and mentorship to students, helping 90% of them achieve their academic goals.

Achievements :

- Recognized as 'Teacher of the Year' for exceptional contributions to student success and curriculum development."

Conclusion

Detailing your work experience effectively is crucial for showcasing your professional journey and achievements on LinkedIn. By using keywords to enhance visibility, structuring your experience for clarity and impact, and leveraging tools like ChatGPT for creativity and efficiency, you can create a compelling and professional work experience section. This not only enhances your LinkedIn profile but also increases your chances of attracting the right opportunities and advancing your career.

Chapter 5

SHOWCASING SKILLS AND ENDORSEMENTS

Selecting Relevant Skills : Choosing Skills That Highlight Your Strengths

The skills section of your LinkedIn profile is a powerful tool for showcasing your professional abilities and expertise. It allows you to highlight the areas where you excel and provides a quick snapshot of your qualifications to potential employers, clients, and collaborators. Selecting relevant skills is crucial for creating a compelling profile that accurately represents your strengths and enhances your visibility on the platform.

Why Selecting Relevant Skills Matters

1. First Impressions : The skills section is one of the first things recruiters and hiring managers look at when reviewing your profile. Highlighting the right skills can make a strong first impression.

2. Searchability : LinkedIn's search algorithms use skills as a key factor in search results. Including relevant skills increases your chances of appearing in searches for specific qualifications.

3. Credibility : Skills backed by endorsements from colleagues and peers add credibility to your profile. They serve as a form of social proof that you possess the expertise you claim.

How to Select Relevant Skills

Choosing the right skills involves understanding your professional strengths, the demands of your industry, and the expectations of potential employers. Here's how to select relevant skills effectively :

1. Identify Your Core Competencies

Reflect on Your Experience : Consider your past roles and responsibilities. What tasks and projects have you excelled at? What skills did you frequently use?

List Your Achievements : Think about your key achievements and the skills that enabled you to accomplish them. For example, if you successfully led a team project, leadership and project management might be core skills.

Seek Feedback : Ask colleagues, supervisors, or mentors for their input on your strengths. They might highlight skills you haven't considered.

2. Research Industry Trends

Analyze Job Descriptions : Look at job postings for positions similar to yours. Identify common terms and phrases that employers use.

Industry Trends : Stay updated on industry trends and terminology. Use terms that are current and widely recognized in your field.

Join Professional Groups : Participate in LinkedIn groups relevant to your industry. Discussions often reveal the skills that are in high demand.

3. Prioritize Transferable Skills

Versatile Skills : Highlight skills that are valuable across multiple roles and industries, such as communication, problem-solving, and leadership. These skills demonstrate your ability to adapt and succeed in various environments.

Technical Skills : Include any technical skills that are essential to your profession. For example, construction professionals should list project management tools, while musicians might list proficiency with specific instruments or software.

Soft Skills : Don't overlook soft skills. Abilities like teamwork, creativity, and emotional intelligence are increasingly valued by employers.

4. Align with Your Career Goals

Current Role : Ensure that the skills you list are relevant to your current role and responsibilities. This demonstrates your proficiency in your current job.

Future Aspirations : Think about where you want to go in your career. If you're aiming for a leadership position, include skills like strategic planning and team management.

5. Update Regularly

Ongoing Learning : As you acquire new skills through work, courses, or personal projects, update your LinkedIn profile accordingly. This shows that you are committed to continuous learning and professional development.

Relevance Check : Periodically review your skills list to ensure it remains relevant to your career path and industry trends. Remove outdated or less relevant skills to keep your profile focused.

Examples of Skills by Industry

Construction

Project Manager

- Project Management

- Construction Planning

- Budgeting and Cost Control

- Safety Compliance

- Team Leadership

Civil Engineer

- Structural Analysis

- AutoCAD

- Project Scheduling

- Site Inspection

- Environmental Impact Assessment

Music

Music Producer

- Music Production

- Sound Engineering

- Mixing and Mastering

- Pro Tools

- Studio Recording

Musician

- Instrument Proficiency (e.g., Guitar, Piano)

- Music Theory

- Performance

- Composition

- Live Sound

Jewellery

Jewelry Designer

- Jewelry Design
- CAD (Computer-Aided Design)
- Gemology
- Metalworking
- Trend Analysis

Jeweler

- Stone Setting
- Jewelry Repair
- Metal Soldering
- Engraving
- Quality Control

Carpentry

Carpenter

- Woodworking
- Blueprint Reading
- Cabinet Making
- Finish Carpentry
- Furniture Design

Cabinet Maker

- Cabinet Construction
- Joinery
- CNC Machining
- Veneering
- Custom Design

Archeology

Archeologist

- Excavation Techniques
- Artifact Analysis

- Historical Research
- GIS (Geographic Information Systems)
- Cultural Resource Management

Conservation Specialist

- Artifact Conservation
- Preservation Techniques
- Analytical Methods
- Field Surveying
- Museum Practices

Best Practices for Listing Skills on LinkedIn

1. Be Specific : Instead of listing general skills like "management," be specific with skills like "project management" or "team leadership."

2. Use Industry Terminology : Use the language and terminology common in your industry to describe your skills. This makes your profile more relatable to industry professionals.

3. Order of Importance : List your most important and relevant skills first. This ensures they are immediately visible to anyone viewing your profile.

4. Skill Endorsements : Encourage colleagues and peers to endorse your skills. Endorsements add credibility and increase the likelihood that your profile will appear in relevant searches.

5. Skill Assessments : Take LinkedIn's skill assessments to validate your expertise. Passing these assessments adds a verified badge to your profile, enhancing your credibility.

Leveraging ChatGPT to Select and Highlight Skills

Using AI tools like ChatGPT can assist you in selecting and articulating your skills effectively. Here's how to leverage ChatGPT for this purpose :

Why Use ChatGPT

1. Creativity : ChatGPT can provide creative ways to describe your skills, making them more compelling.

2. Efficiency : It can quickly generate a list of relevant skills based on your job role and industry.

3. Clarity and Precision : ChatGPT helps articulate your skills clearly and precisely, enhancing your profile's readability.

Effective Prompts for ChatGPT

To get the best results, use clear and specific prompts. Here are some examples :

1. General Skill Identification

- "I am a carpenter specializing in custom furniture. What skills should I highlight on my LinkedIn profile?"

- "I am a jewelry designer. Can you suggest the most important skills to include in my LinkedIn profile?"

2. Crafting Skill Descriptions

- "How can I describe my skill in project management for my LinkedIn profile as a construction project manager?"

- "Help me write a compelling description for my expertise in sound engineering as a music producer."

3. Increasing Endorsements

- "What strategies can I use to increase endorsements for my skills in woodwork and blueprint reading on LinkedIn?"

- "How can I encourage my colleagues to endorse my skills in gemology and jewelry design?"

Sample Outputs from ChatGPT

1. For a Carpenter

- Suggested Skills : Woodworking, Blueprint Reading, Cabinet Making, Finish Carpentry, Furniture Design

- Description : "Proficient in woodworking and blueprint reading, I specialize in creating custom furniture with meticulous attention to detail. My expertise includes cabinet making and finish carpentry, ensuring high-quality craftsmanship and precision in every project."

2. For a Jewelry Designer

- Suggested Skills : Jewelry Design, CAD, Gemology, Metalworking, Trend Analysis

- Description : "Experienced jewelry designer skilled in CAD and gemology, I create unique and trend-setting pieces. My expertise in metalworking and stone setting ensures each design is both beautiful and durable, reflecting the latest trends and highest standards of craftsmanship."

3. Strategies for Increasing Endorsements

- Direct Request : "Reach out to colleagues and mentors with a personalized message requesting endorsements for specific skills. Highlight shared projects to remind them of your contributions."

- Give Endorsements : "Endorse the skills of your connections genuinely. Often, they will reciprocate by endorsing your skills in return."

- Engage on LinkedIn : "Stay active on LinkedIn by participating in discussions, sharing professional updates, and engaging with your network's content. Increased visibility can lead to more endorsements."

Conclusion

Selecting relevant skills and securing endorsements are critical aspects of creating a compelling LinkedIn profile. By identifying your core competencies, researching industry trends, prioritizing transferable skills, and aligning your skills with your career goals, you can effectively showcase your strengths. Utilizing tools like ChatGPT can further enhance this process by providing creative and precise skill descriptions and strategies for increasing endorsements. A well-curated skills section, backed by endorsements, not only improves your profile's visibility but also demonstrates your expertise and readiness for new opportunities.

Chapter 6

BUILDING A PROFESSIONAL NETWORK

Connecting with Others : How to Grow Your LinkedIn Network

Building a robust LinkedIn network is essential for expanding your professional reach, discovering new opportunities, and enhancing your career prospects. Growing your network effectively requires a strategic approach to connecting with the right people and fostering meaningful relationships. Here's how to do it :

Why Building a Network Matters

1. Opportunities : A strong network can lead to job offers, collaborations, partnerships, and other professional opportunities.

2. Knowledge Sharing : Connecting with others allows you to exchange ideas, stay informed about industry trends, and gain new insights.

3. Support System : Your network can provide support, advice, and mentorship, helping you navigate your career path more effectively.

Strategies for Connecting with Others

1. Personalize Connection Requests

Tailored Messages : Avoid sending generic connection requests. Personalize each message to explain why you want to connect and how you can mutually benefit from the connection.

Example :

"Hi [Name], I came across your profile and was impressed by your experience in [industry/field]. I'm currently working on [related project/role], and I'd love to connect and possibly share insights. Looking forward to connecting!"

2. Utilize Alumni Networks

Common Ground : Connect with alumni from your educational institutions. Shared experiences can provide a strong foundation for building professional relationships.

LinkedIn Alumni Tool : Use LinkedIn's Alumni tool to find and connect with former classmates and colleagues from your university.

3. Join LinkedIn Groups

Industry Groups : Join groups related to your industry or interests. Participate in discussions, share content, and connect with group members who share similar professional interests.

Active Participation : Be active in group discussions to increase your visibility and establish yourself as a knowledgeable and engaged professional.

4. Engage with Content

Comment and Share : Engage with posts from your connections by liking, commenting, and sharing. This keeps you visible in your network and can lead to new connections.

Create Content : Regularly share your own content, such as articles, insights, and updates. This showcases your expertise and attracts like-minded professionals to connect with you.

5. Attend Virtual Events and Webinars

Networking Opportunities : Participate in virtual events and webinars relevant to your field. These events often provide networking opportunities and allow you to connect with speakers and attendees.

Follow-Up : After the event, follow up with new connections by sending personalized messages referencing the event and your conversation.

6. Leverage Second-Degree Connections

Introductions : Use your existing connections to get introduced to second-degree connections. This can be an effective way to expand your network with trusted recommendations.

Example :

"Hi [Connection's Name], I noticed you're connected with [Second-Degree Connection's Name], who has experience in [industry/field]. Would you be able to introduce us? I'd love to discuss [specific topic or project]. Thank you!"

Engaging with Connections : Tips for Maintaining Professional Relationships

Building a network is just the first step. Maintaining and nurturing those connections is crucial for long-term professional success. Here's how to engage with your LinkedIn connections effectively :

Why Engagement Matters

1. Relationship Building : Regular engagement helps build stronger, more meaningful relationships.

2. Staying Top of Mind : Consistent interaction keeps you visible to your network, increasing the likelihood of opportunities coming your way.

3. Trust and Credibility : Engaging with your network regularly builds trust and establishes you as a credible and reliable professional.

Strategies for Engaging with Connections

1. Regular Check-Ins

Personal Messages : Periodically send personalized messages to your connections. Ask about their current projects, share updates about your work, and find out how you can support each other.

Example :

"Hi [Name], it's been a while since we last connected. How have you been? I recently started working on [project/role] and thought it might be interesting to you. Let's catch up soon!"

2. Congratulate and Celebrate

Acknowledging Milestones : Congratulate your connections on their achievements, such as promotions, job changes, or work anniversaries. This shows you care and are paying attention to their career progress.

Example :

"Hi [Name], congratulations on your new role at [Company]! Wishing you great success in this exciting new chapter. Let's catch up soon to hear all about it."

3. Share Valuable Content

Informative Articles : Share articles, reports, and insights that are relevant to your connections' interests and industry. This positions you as a resourceful and knowledgeable professional.

Example :

"Hi [Name], I came across this article about [topic] and thought you might find it interesting. It aligns well with our recent conversation on [related topic]."

4. Offer Help and Support

Proactive Assistance : Offer your help and support when appropriate. This could be in the form of advice, introductions, or sharing resources.

Example :

"Hi [Name], I noticed you're exploring opportunities in [industry/field]. I'd be happy to introduce you to a contact of mine who might be able to assist. Let me know if that would be helpful!"

5. Engage with Their Content

Comments and Likes : Regularly engage with your connections' posts by liking, commenting, and sharing. This shows your support and keeps the conversation going.

Example :

"Great post, [Name]! Your insights on [topic] are spot on. Thanks for sharing!"

6. Schedule Networking Calls

Virtual Coffee Chats : Schedule periodic virtual coffee chats or catch-up calls with your key connections. These informal conversations can strengthen your relationship and uncover new opportunities for collaboration.

Example :

"Hi [Name], it's been a while since we last spoke. Would you be open to a virtual coffee chat next week to catch up and discuss potential collaboration opportunities?"

Examples of Networking Success Stories : Case Studies of Effective Networking

Real-life examples can illustrate the power of effective networking and provide inspiration for your own efforts. Here are some networking success stories that demonstrate the impact of building and maintaining a professional network on LinkedIn :

Success Story 1 : The Power of Alumni Connections

Background : Jane, a marketing professional, wanted to transition from a corporate role to a startup environment. She had limited connections in the startup world but was determined to make the switch.

Strategy : Jane utilized LinkedIn's Alumni tool to find graduates from her university working in startups. She sent personalized connection requests, referencing their shared educational background and expressing her interest in learning more about their career paths.

Outcome : Through her alumni network, Jane connected with a startup founder who was also an alum. They had several conversations, and the founder eventually offered Jane a role as a marketing director at his startup. Jane's strategic use of her alumni network facilitated a successful career transition.

Success Story 2 : Leveraging LinkedIn Groups

Background : Tom, a software developer, was looking to expand his freelance business. He needed to connect with potential clients and other developers to grow his network.

Strategy : Tom joined several LinkedIn groups related to software development and freelance work. He actively participated in discussions, shared his expertise, and provided valuable insights to group members.

Outcome : Tom's active participation in LinkedIn groups led to several new client inquiries and collaborations with other developers. By positioning himself as a knowledgeable and engaged professional, Tom significantly expanded his freelance business and network.

Success Story 3 : Engaging with Content

Background : Sarah, a financial analyst, wanted to raise her profile within the finance industry and attract new career opportunities.

Strategy : Sarah regularly shared insightful articles and industry reports on LinkedIn. She also engaged with content posted by industry leaders, commenting thoughtfully and contributing to discussions.

Outcome : Sarah's consistent engagement with industry content caught the attention of several recruiters and hiring managers. She was approached with multiple job offers and eventually accepted a senior analyst position at a top financial firm. Her proactive content engagement significantly boosted her visibility and career prospects.

Success Story 4 : Virtual Networking at Events

Background : Mike, an HR professional, was looking to connect with other HR leaders to share best practices and explore potential collaborations.

Strategy : Mike attended several virtual HR conferences and webinars. After each event, he reached out to speakers and participants on LinkedIn, referencing the event and expressing his interest in continuing the conversation.

Outcome : Mike's follow-up messages led to numerous meaningful connections. He collaborated on a whitepaper with one of the speakers and joined a think tank with other HR professionals he met at the events. Virtual networking significantly enhanced Mike's professional network and opened up new collaboration opportunities.

Conclusion

Building and maintaining a professional network on LinkedIn is essential for career growth and professional development. By strategically connecting with others, actively engaging with your network, and leveraging various networking opportunities, you can create a robust and valuable professional network. Real-life success stories demonstrate the tangible benefits of effective networking and provide actionable insights for your own networking efforts. Embrace these strategies to enhance your LinkedIn network and unlock new opportunities for career advancement.

Chapter 7

RECOMMENDATIONS AND TESTIMONIALS

Requesting Recommendations : How to Ask for and Receive Quality Recommendations

Receiving high-quality recommendations on LinkedIn can significantly enhance your profile by providing third-party validation of your skills and accomplishments. Recommendations add credibility and help potential employers, clients, and collaborators understand the impact of your work from another perspective. Here's how to effectively request and receive quality recommendations :

Why Recommendations Matter

1. Credibility : Recommendations provide social proof that you possess the skills and experience you claim.

2. Differentiation : A strong recommendation can set you apart from others with similar profiles.

3. Networking : Asking for recommendations can strengthen your relationships and keep you top of mind with past colleagues and supervisors.

Strategies for Requesting Recommendations

1. Identify the Right People

Choose Relevant Contacts : Request recommendations from colleagues, supervisors, clients, and collaborators who can speak specifically about your skills and contributions.

Diverse Perspectives : Aim for a mix of recommendations from different roles and projects to provide a well-rounded view of your capabilities.

2. Personalize Your Request

Be Specific : Clearly explain why you are asking for a recommendation and what specific skills or experiences you'd like the person to highlight.

Example Request :

"Hi [Name], I hope you're doing well! I'm reaching out to see if you would be willing to write a recommendation for me. Specifically, I'd love it if you could highlight our collaboration on [project/task] and my skills in [specific area]. Your insights would be invaluable. Thank you!"

3. Provide Guidance

Offer Details : Make it easy for the person to write the recommendation by providing key points or achievements you'd like them to mention.

Example :

"To help with the recommendation, you might want to mention our work on [project], where we achieved [specific result], and how I contributed by [specific actions]."

4. Be Gracious and Patient

Show Appreciation : Thank the person for considering your request, regardless of their response. Follow up with a thank-you message once the recommendation is written.

Example :

"Thank you so much for taking the time to write this recommendation, [Name]. I truly appreciate your support and kind words!"

5. Timing and Relevance

Recent Interactions : Request recommendations shortly after completing a project or collaboration when the details are fresh.

Professional Milestones : Use milestones like promotions, job changes, or the end of significant projects as opportunities to request recommendations.

Writing Recommendations for Others : Best Practices for Writing Recommendations

Writing recommendations for others on LinkedIn is an excellent way to support your colleagues, strengthen professional relationships, and demonstrate your appreciation for their work. Here's how to write impactful recommendations :

Why Writing Recommendations Matters

1. Relationship Building : Writing recommendations strengthens your professional relationships and encourages reciprocity.

2. Visibility : Your name appears on the profiles of those you recommend, increasing your visibility within their network.

3. Reputation : Thoughtful recommendations reflect well on you as a supportive and engaged professional.

Best Practices for Writing Recommendations

1. Be Specific and Detailed

Concrete Examples : Use specific examples to illustrate the person's skills and accomplishments. This makes your recommendation more credible and impactful.

Example :

"During our time together at XYZ Corp, Jane led the redesign of our software platform, which resulted in a 50% increase in user engagement. Her creativity and attention to detail were instrumental in the project's success."

2. Highlight Key Strengths

Focus on Strengths : Identify the person's key strengths and how they contributed to the team or project. Highlighting these strengths provides valuable insights for potential employers.

Example :

"Tom's expertise in solar energy technology and his analytical skills helped our team identify cost-saving opportunities that resulted in a 20% reduction in energy expenses."

3. Include Soft Skills

Soft Skills Matter : Mention soft skills such as teamwork, communication, and leadership. These are often as important as technical skills in a professional setting.

Example :

"Susan is not only a talented engineer but also a great team player. Her ability to communicate effectively and collaborate with different departments made her an invaluable asset to our team."

4. Be Authentic and Positive

Genuine Praise : Ensure your recommendation is authentic and based on your true experience working with the person. Avoid generic or overly exaggerated statements.

Example :

"Mark's dedication and work ethic are truly commendable. He consistently goes above and beyond to deliver high-quality results and is always willing to help others."

5. Structure and Clarity

Organized Structure : Use a clear structure with an introduction, body, and conclusion. This makes your recommendation easy to read and understand.

Example :

"In the two years I worked with Emily at ABC Inc., she demonstrated exceptional leadership and project management skills. She successfully led our team to complete several high-impact projects, all delivered on time and within budget. I highly recommend Emily for any leadership role."

Examples of Strong Recommendations : Analysis of Impactful Recommendations

Analyzing strong recommendations can provide insights into what makes them effective. Here are examples of impactful recommendations from different industries, along with an analysis of why they work well :

Software Technology

Recommendation for a Software Developer :

"John is one of the most talented software engineers I've had the pleasure of working with. At XYZ Tech, he played a pivotal role in developing our flagship product, which now serves millions of users. His proficiency in Java and Python, combined with his problem-solving skills, consistently delivered innovative solutions to complex challenges. John's ability to work seamlessly in a team and his dedication to continuous learning make him a standout professional. I highly recommend John for any software development role."

Analysis :

- Specific Skills : Highlights John's proficiency in Java and Python.

- Impact : Mentions the scale of the product and John's role in its success.

- Soft Skills : Notes his teamwork and dedication to learning.

- Overall Impression : Provides a comprehensive view of John's capabilities and impact.

Solar Energy

Recommendation for a Solar Energy Specialist :

"Lisa's expertise in solar energy is unparalleled. During her tenure at ABC Solar, she spearheaded a project that increased our energy output by 30% within six months. Her strategic thinking, technical skills, and deep understanding of renewable energy were key drivers of this success. Lisa is also a fantastic leader who fosters a collaborative and innovative team environment. I have no doubt she will continue to excel in her career and highly recommend her for any senior role in renewable energy."

Analysis :

- Quantifiable Results : Provides specific metrics (30% increase in energy output) to illustrate Lisa's impact.

- Key Strengths : Highlights her strategic thinking, technical skills, and understanding of renewable energy.

- Leadership : Mentions her leadership qualities and ability to foster a positive team environment.

- Recommendation : Strong endorsement for senior roles, indicating confidence in her continued success.

Cement Manufacturing

Recommendation for a Production Manager :

"Emma is an exceptional production manager whose expertise has significantly improved our manufacturing process at XYZ Cement. Her ability to optimize production schedules and implement efficiency measures resulted in a 15% increase in productivity and a 10% reduction in costs. Emma's attention to detail and commitment to quality have set new standards for our operations. I highly recommend Emma for any production management role."

Analysis :

- Specific Achievements : Highlights Emma's role in increasing productivity and reducing costs.

- Soft Skills : Emphasizes her attention to detail and commitment to quality.

- Impact on Operations : Notes her broader impact on setting new standards for operations.

- Recommendation : Strongly endorses her for production management roles, indicating trust in her abilities.

Textiles

Recommendation for a Textile Designer :

"David is an outstanding textile designer whose innovative designs have set trends in the fashion industry. At ABC Textiles, he developed several new fabric patterns that became bestsellers. His creativity, combined with his deep understanding of textile materials and production processes, has made a significant impact on our product line. David's ability to collaborate with designers and production teams ensures that his designs are both beautiful and practical. I highly recommend David for any design role."

Analysis :

- Creative Impact : Highlights David's role in developing bestselling fabric patterns.

- Technical Skills : Emphasizes his understanding of textile materials and production processes.

- Collaboration : Notes his ability to work well with designers and production teams.

- Recommendation : Strongly endorses him for design roles, showcasing his creativity and technical expertise.

Cellphone Manufacturing

Recommendation for a Product Manager :

"Sarah is an exceptional product manager whose strategic vision has driven the success of several key projects at XYZ Mobile. She successfully led the development and launch of our latest smartphone, which received rave reviews and exceeded sales targets. Sarah's market analysis skills and customer-focused approach were instrumental in shaping the product's features and positioning. Her leadership and project management skills are truly impressive. I highly recommend Sarah for any senior product management role."

Analysis :

- Specific Achievements : Highlights Sarah's role in the successful launch of a smartphone.

- Key Strengths : Emphasizes her market analysis skills and customer-focused approach.

- Leadership : Notes her leadership and project management abilities.

- Recommendation : Strongly endorses her for senior product management roles, indicating trust in her strategic vision and execution.

Conclusion

Recommendations and testimonials on LinkedIn provide invaluable third-party validation of your skills and accomplishments. By strategically requesting recommendations, writing thoughtful endorsements for others, and understanding the elements of strong recommendations, you can significantly enhance your LinkedIn profile. This not only boosts your credibility but also opens up new professional opportunities. Use the strategies and examples provided to build a compelling collection of recommendations that showcase your expertise and professional impact.

Chapter 8

LINKEDIN FOR JOB SEEKERS

Job Search Strategies : How to Use LinkedIn to Find Job Opportunities

LinkedIn is a powerful tool for job seekers, offering a myriad of opportunities to connect with potential employers, discover job openings, and showcase your professional brand. To leverage LinkedIn effectively in your job search, you need to be strategic and proactive. Here are some comprehensive strategies to help you navigate LinkedIn and find the right job opportunities :

Why LinkedIn Matters for Job Seekers

1. Vast Network : LinkedIn connects you with professionals from all over the world, expanding your reach and access to job opportunities.

2. Job Listings : Many companies post job openings exclusively on LinkedIn, making it a crucial platform for discovering roles that might not be advertised elsewhere.

3. Recruiter Access : Recruiters actively use LinkedIn to find candidates, making it essential to have a well-optimized profile.

Strategies for Job Searching on LinkedIn

1. Set Up Job Alerts

Customized Alerts: Use LinkedIn's job alerts to receive notifications about new job postings that match your criteria. Customize these alerts based on job title, location, industry, and company.

Example :

"Create a job alert for 'Marketing Manager' positions in 'New York City' within the 'Tech Industry.' Set the alert to notify you daily."

2. Utilize LinkedIn's Job Search Function

Advanced Filters : Use LinkedIn's advanced search filters to narrow down job listings based on specific criteria like experience level, company size, and job type (full-time, part-time, remote).

Example :

"Filter job search results to show 'Entry-Level' 'Software Engineer' roles in 'San Francisco' with 'Remote' work options."

3. Leverage Your Network

Reach Out : Inform your network that you are job hunting. Reach out to former colleagues, mentors, and connections in your desired industry for advice, referrals, and job leads.

Example :

"Hi [Name], I hope you're doing well. I'm currently exploring new opportunities in digital marketing and would love any advice or referrals you might have. Thank you!"

4. Engage with Company Pages

Follow Companies : Follow companies you're interested in to stay updated on their job postings, news, and updates. Engage with their content to show your interest and stay visible.

Example :

"Follow 'XYZ Corp' and engage with their posts by liking, commenting, and sharing. Stay informed about their job openings and company news."

5. Join Industry Groups

Participate in Groups : Join LinkedIn groups related to your industry or career interests. Participate in discussions, share insights, and network with other professionals.

Example :

"Join the 'Digital Marketing Professionals' group, contribute to discussions, and connect with members who share job leads and industry insights."

6. Use LinkedIn's "Open to Work" Feature

Open to Work : Enable the "Open to Work" feature on your profile to let recruiters know you are actively seeking job opportunities. Customize the settings to specify the types of roles you are interested in.

Example :

"Activate the 'Open to Work' feature and select job preferences such as 'Marketing Manager,' 'Remote,' 'Full-Time,' and 'Tech Industry.'"

Optimizing Your Profile for Recruiters : Tips to Make Your Profile Attractive to Recruiters

To attract recruiters on LinkedIn, you need to ensure your profile is complete, compelling, and optimized for searchability. Here are detailed tips to make your profile stand out to recruiters :

Why Optimization Matters

1. Visibility : An optimized profile increases your chances of appearing in recruiters' search results.

2. First Impressions : A well-crafted profile makes a strong first impression, encouraging recruiters to learn more about you.

3. Credibility : A comprehensive profile with endorsements and recommendations adds credibility and demonstrates your professional competence.

Tips for Optimizing Your Profile

1. Complete Your Profile

Profile Completeness : Ensure every section of your profile is filled out, including your headline, summary, work experience, skills, and education. LinkedIn profiles with complete information rank higher in search results.

Example :

"Complete your profile by adding detailed descriptions for each job role, listing relevant skills, and filling out your education history."

2. Craft a Compelling Headline

Keyword-Rich Headline : Create a headline that includes relevant keywords and clearly describes your professional identity. This makes your profile more discoverable and attractive to recruiters.

Example :

"Digital Marketing Manager | SEO Specialist | Content Strategist | Driving Growth Through Data-Driven Marketing"

3. Write an Engaging Summary

Professional Story : Use your summary to tell your professional story, highlight your key achievements, and showcase your skills. Incorporate keywords naturally to improve searchability.

Example :

"Passionate digital marketing professional with over 10 years of experience in SEO, content strategy, and social media marketing. Proven track record of increasing online engagement by 200% through innovative and data-driven campaigns. Seeking new opportunities to drive growth in a dynamic and forward-thinking company."

4. Highlight Key Achievements

Quantify Success : In your work experience section, highlight your key achievements and quantify your successes with numbers and metrics. This demonstrates your impact and effectiveness.

Example :

"Led a cross-functional team to launch a new product, resulting in a 35% increase in sales and a 50% improvement in customer satisfaction ratings."

5. Showcase Relevant Skills

Endorsed Skills : List relevant skills that match the job roles you are seeking. Ensure these skills are endorsed by colleagues to add credibility.

Example :

"SEO, Content Marketing, Social Media Strategy, Google Analytics, Project Management"

6. Request Recommendations

Quality Recommendations : Request recommendations from colleagues, supervisors, and clients who can speak to your skills and accomplishments. These add credibility and depth to your profile.

Example :

"Received a recommendation from a former supervisor highlighting your leadership skills and successful project outcomes."

7. Use a Professional Photo

Profile Picture : Use a high-quality, professional photo that reflects your industry standards. A good profile picture makes your profile more approachable and trustworthy.

Example :

"A professional headshot with a clean background and appropriate attire for your industry."

Examples of Job Seeker Profiles : Case Studies of Successful Job Seeker Profiles

Analyzing successful job seeker profiles can provide valuable insights into what makes them effective. Here are case studies of job seekers who optimized their LinkedIn profiles and achieved their career goals :

Case Study 1 : Marketing Professional

Profile Summary :

"Experienced Marketing Manager with a decade of success in driving digital campaigns and increasing brand visibility. Skilled in SEO, content strategy, and social media management. Proven ability to lead cross-functional teams and deliver exceptional results. Open to opportunities in innovative companies looking to enhance their digital marketing efforts."

Key Elements :

- Compelling Headline : "Marketing Manager | Digital Strategist | SEO Expert | Driving Engagement and Growth"

- Detailed Experience : Each role includes specific achievements, such as "Increased website traffic by 150% through targeted SEO strategies."

- Endorsed Skills : SEO, Content Marketing, Social Media Strategy, Google Analytics

- Recommendations : Recommendations from former supervisors praising leadership and strategic thinking.

Outcome : Attracted multiple interview offers and secured a senior marketing position at a leading tech company.

Case Study 2 : Software Engineer

Profile Summary :

"Passionate Software Engineer with 7+ years of experience in full-stack development. Expertise in JavaScript, React, Node.js, and cloud technologies. Proven track record of building scalable web applications that enhance user experience. Seeking new opportunities to leverage my skills in innovative and challenging projects."

Key Elements :

- Compelling Headline : "Software Engineer | Full-Stack Developer | JavaScript, React, Node.js | Building Scalable Solutions"

- Detailed Experience : Highlighted specific projects and technologies used, such as "Developed a real-time data visualization tool using React and D3.js."

- Endorsed Skills : JavaScript, React, Node.js, AWS, Agile Methodologies

- Recommendations : Positive recommendations from team leads and project managers highlighting technical skills and teamwork.

Outcome : Received several job offers and accepted a role as a Senior Software Engineer at a fast-growing startup.

Case Study 3 : Financial Analyst

Profile Summary :

"Detail-oriented Financial Analyst with over 5 years of experience in financial modeling, data analysis, and investment strategy. Adept at providing actionable insights to drive business growth and improve financial performance. Looking for opportunities to contribute to a dynamic finance team and support strategic decision-making."

Key Elements :

- Compelling Headline : "Financial Analyst | Data-Driven Decision Maker | Financial Modeling | Investment Strategy"

- Detailed Experience : Included specific metrics, such as "Developed financial models that improved forecasting accuracy by 25%."

- Endorsed Skills : Financial Modeling, Data Analysis, Excel, SQL, Risk Management

- Recommendations : Recommendations from supervisors and colleagues highlighting analytical skills and impact on financial performance.

Outcome : Secured a Financial Analyst position at a major investment firm within three months of optimizing the profile.

Case Study 4 : Healthcare Administrator

Profile Summary :

"Experienced Healthcare Administrator with a strong background in hospital operations and patient care management. Proven ability to implement efficient processes and improve patient satisfaction. Seeking to leverage my skills in a leadership role at a forward-thinking healthcare organization."

Key Elements :

- Compelling Headline : "Healthcare Administrator | Operations Management | Patient Care Excellence | Process Improvement"

- Detailed Experience : Highlighted specific achievements, such as "Implemented a new scheduling system that reduced patient wait times by 30%."

- Endorsed Skills : Healthcare Management, Operations Management, Patient Care, Strategic Planning

- Recommendations : Strong recommendations from hospital

directors and peers emphasizing leadership and operational efficiency.

Outcome : Received multiple interviews and accepted a senior administrative role at a renowned hospital.

Conclusion

LinkedIn is an indispensable tool for job seekers, offering numerous opportunities to connect with potential employers and showcase your professional brand. By employing strategic job search techniques, optimizing your profile for recruiters, and learning from successful case studies, you can significantly enhance your LinkedIn presence and improve your chances of finding the right job. Implement these strategies to leverage LinkedIn effectively and achieve your career goals.

Chapter 9

LINKEDIN FOR RECRUITERS

Candidate Search Strategies

LinkedIn is an invaluable tool for recruiters seeking to find the best talent. With its extensive network of professionals across various industries, it offers numerous features and strategies to optimize the candidate search process. Here's how to effectively utilize LinkedIn for candidate searches :

Why LinkedIn Matters for Recruiters

1. Vast Talent Pool : Access to millions of professionals from diverse industries and locations.

2. Advanced Search Tools : Powerful search capabilities to narrow down candidates based on specific criteria.

3. Networking : Ability to connect with passive candidates who may not be actively job searching.

Strategies for Effective Candidate Searches

1. Utilize Advanced Search Filters

Refine Searches : Use LinkedIn's advanced search filters to narrow down candidates by location, industry, current company, past company, school, and more.

Example :

"Search for 'Software Engineers' in 'San Francisco' who have worked at 'Google' and graduated from 'Stanford University.'"

2. Leverage Boolean Search

Boolean Operators : Use Boolean search techniques to refine your candidate search further. Combine keywords with operators like AND, OR, and NOT to find the most relevant profiles.

Example :

"Search for 'Project Manager AND Agile AND NOT Junior' to find experienced project managers with agile expertise."

3. Explore LinkedIn Recruiter

LinkedIn Recruiter : Utilize LinkedIn Recruiter, a specialized tool designed for recruiters. It offers enhanced search capabilities, InMail credits for direct messaging, and the ability to organize and manage candidate pipelines.

Example :

"Use LinkedIn Recruiter to set up projects for different roles, track candidate interactions, and send personalized InMail messages to potential candidates."

4. Set Up Job Alerts

Automated Alerts : Set up job alerts for specific roles and receive notifications when new candidates match your criteria. This keeps you updated on potential new hires without constant manual searches.

Example :

"Create a job alert for 'Marketing Director' positions in 'New York City' and receive daily notifications of new candidates."

5. Engage with Professional Groups

Join Groups : Participate in LinkedIn groups relevant to the industries you recruit for. This helps you identify active professionals and engage with potential candidates.

Example :

"Join the 'HR Professionals' group to connect with experienced HR managers and share insights."

6. Utilize Company Followers

Company Page Insights : Review the list of followers on your company's LinkedIn page. These individuals have shown interest in your company and might be open to job opportunities.

Example :

"Reach out to company followers who have relevant experience and invite them to apply for open positions."

Optimizing Profiles for Job Seekers

Just as job seekers need to optimize their profiles to attract recruiters, recruiters should also optimize their profiles to attract top talent. A well-optimized recruiter profile can enhance your credibility and make candidates more willing to engage with you.

Why Optimizing Your Profile Matters

1. Trust and Credibility : A professional and detailed profile builds trust with potential candidates.

2. Visibility : An optimized profile improves your visibility in LinkedIn searches.

3. Engagement : A compelling profile encourages candidates to connect and engage with you.

Tips for Optimizing Your Profile

1. Professional Headline

Clear and Descriptive : Your headline should clearly describe your role and expertise. Include relevant keywords to enhance searchability.

Example :

"Senior Technical Recruiter | Specializing in Software Development and Engineering Roles"

2. Comprehensive Summary

Engaging Summary : Write a detailed summary that outlines your experience, recruiting philosophy, and the types of roles you specialize in. Highlight your achievements and what candidates can expect when working with you.

Example :

"With over 10 years of experience in technical recruiting, I specialize in connecting top software engineering talent with innovative companies. My goal is to create a seamless and positive recruitment experience, ensuring both clients and candidates find the perfect match. Passionate about technology and dedicated to building strong relationships, I am here to help you take the next step in your career."

3. Detailed Experience

Specific Achievements : List your roles and responsibilities, focusing on key achievements and successful placements. Use quantifiable metrics to demonstrate your impact.

Example :

"Placed over 100 software engineers in high-growth tech startups, achieving a 95% retention rate within the first year."

4. Showcase Skills and Endorsements

Relevant Skills : Highlight skills relevant to your recruiting expertise, such as talent acquisition, sourcing, interviewing, and candidate relationship management. Ensure these skills are endorsed by colleagues.

Example :

"Talent Acquisition, Candidate Sourcing, Technical Recruiting, Interviewing, Relationship Management"

5. Recommendations

Quality Recommendations : Request recommendations from colleagues, hiring managers, and candidates you have placed. These testimonials add credibility and provide social proof of your expertise.

Example :

"John is an exceptional recruiter who truly understands the needs of both candidates and clients. His ability to match the right talent with the right opportunities is unparalleled."

6. Engage with Content

Share and Comment : Regularly share industry insights, job postings, and company news. Engage with content posted by others to increase your visibility and demonstrate your active involvement in the industry.

Example :

"Share articles on the latest trends in technical recruiting, comment on posts from industry leaders, and share updates on successful placements."

Examples of Recruiter Profiles Across Various Industries

Analyzing effective recruiter profiles can provide valuable insights into what makes them stand out. Here are examples of well-optimized recruiter profiles from different industries, highlighting their strengths and best practices :

Example 1 : Technology Recruiter

Profile Summary :

"Experienced Technical Recruiter with a focus on sourcing and placing top software engineering talent. With a background in software development, I understand the technical skills and qualities required for success in the tech industry. Dedicated to creating a positive candidate experience and building long-term relationships with clients. Let's connect to discuss how I can help you find your next career opportunity or top talent."

Key Elements :

- Professional Headline : "Technical Recruiter | Software Engineering Talent | Candidate Experience Advocate"

- Detailed Experience : "Placed over 150 software engineers and developers in leading tech companies. Expertise in sourcing candidates through advanced search techniques and networking."

- Endorsed Skills : Talent Acquisition, Technical Recruiting, Candidate Sourcing, Relationship Management

- Recommendations : Testimonials from placed candidates and hiring managers praising technical understanding and placement success.

Outcome : High engagement from tech professionals and successful placements in top tech firms.

Example 2 : Healthcare Recruiter

Profile Summary :

"Senior Healthcare Recruiter with 8+ years of experience in placing top healthcare professionals in hospitals and medical centers. Skilled in understanding the unique needs of the healthcare industry and finding the perfect fit for both candidates and employers. Passionate about improving patient care by ensuring that the best talent is in the right roles. Connect with me to explore opportunities in healthcare."

Key Elements :

- Professional Headline : "Senior Healthcare Recruiter | Nursing and Medical Staff Placement | Improving Patient Care"

- Detailed Experience : "Successfully placed over 200 nurses and medical staff in leading healthcare facilities. Developed strong relationships with hospitals and healthcare providers."

- Endorsed Skills : Healthcare Recruiting, Talent Acquisition, Relationship Building, Candidate Sourcing

- Recommendations : Positive feedback from healthcare professionals and hospital administrators highlighting dedication and successful placements.

Outcome : Strong network of healthcare professionals and high success rate in healthcare placements.

Example 3 : Marketing Recruiter

Profile Summary :

"Dynamic Marketing Recruiter with a passion for connecting creative talent with exciting opportunities in the marketing and advertising industry. Over 7 years of experience in sourcing, interviewing, and placing marketing professionals in roles ranging from digital marketing to creative direction. Committed to understanding the unique skills and aspirations of each candidate to ensure the perfect fit."

Key Elements :

- Professional Headline : "Marketing Recruiter | Creative Talent Connector | Digital Marketing and Advertising Roles"

- Detailed Experience : "Placed over 100 marketing professionals in top advertising agencies and marketing departments. Expertise in identifying creative talent and understanding market trends."

- Endorsed Skills : Marketing Recruiting, Creative Talent Acquisition, Interviewing, Market Analysis

- Recommendations : Endorsements from candidates and marketing managers praising matchmaking skills and industry knowledge.

Outcome : Active engagement with the marketing community and successful placements in top marketing roles.

Example 4 : Finance Recruiter

Profile Summary :

"Finance Recruiter with a decade of experience in placing financial analysts, accountants, and executives in leading financial institutions. Strong background in finance and a deep understanding of industry requirements. Dedicated to providing a seamless recruitment process and finding the right fit for both clients and candidates. Let's connect to explore finance career opportunities."

Key Elements :

- Professional Headline : "Finance Recruiter | Placing Top Financial Talent | Analysts, Accountants, and Executives"

- Detailed Experience : "Successfully placed over 150 finance professionals in major financial firms. Skilled in financial analysis, market research, and talent acquisition."

- Endorsed Skills : Financial Recruiting, Talent Acquisition, Market Research, Executive Placement

- Recommendations : Recommendations from financial professionals and executives emphasizing thorough understanding of finance roles and successful placements.

Outcome : Strong reputation in the finance industry and high placement success rate.

Conclusion

LinkedIn offers a powerful platform for recruiters to find and connect with top talent across various industries. By implementing effective candidate search strategies, optimizing recruiter profiles, and learning from successful examples, recruiters can enhance their ability to attract and engage with the best candidates. Utilize these strategies to make the most of LinkedIn's features and build a strong network of professionals that meets your recruiting needs.

Chapter 10

LINKEDIN FOR ENTREPRENEURS AND BUSINESS OWNERS

Creating a Company Page : Step-by-Step Guide to Setting Up a LinkedIn Company Page

A LinkedIn company page is an essential tool for entrepreneurs and business owners to establish their brand's presence, engage with their audience, and attract potential clients, partners, and employees. Here's a comprehensive guide to setting up your LinkedIn company page :

Why a LinkedIn Company Page Matters

1. Brand Visibility : Increases your business's visibility and credibility on a professional platform.

2. Engagement : Allows you to engage directly with followers, share updates, and showcase company culture.

3. Talent Attraction : Helps attract potential employees by showcasing job opportunities and company values.

Step-by-Step Guide to Creating a Company Page

1. Access LinkedIn's Company Page Creation

Navigation : Log into your LinkedIn account, click on the "Work" icon at the top right corner, and select "Create a Company Page" from the dropdown menu.

Example :

"Go to LinkedIn, click on 'Work' in the top navigation bar, and choose 'Create a Company Page' to start the process."

2. Select Page Type

Options : Choose from Small Business, Medium to Large Business, Showcase Page, or Educational Institution. Select the option that best fits your business size and type.

Example :

"Select 'Small Business' if you are a startup or have a small team, or 'Medium to Large Business' if your company is more established."

3. Enter Company Details

Basic Information : Fill in your company name, LinkedIn public URL, website, industry, company size, and company type. Ensure the information is accurate and reflective of your business.

Example :

"Enter your company name, e.g., 'Glamour Cosmetics Ltd.', and create a LinkedIn URL, e.g., linkedin.com/company/glamour-cosmetics."

4. Upload Company Logo and Banner Image

Visual Identity : Upload a high-quality logo and a banner image that represents your brand. The logo should be 300x300 pixels, and the banner image should be 1536x768 pixels.

Example :

"Upload a professional logo and a visually appealing banner that reflects your company's branding and values."

5. Write a Compelling Company Description

Overview : Craft a clear and engaging company description that outlines your mission, values, products/services, and unique selling points. Include relevant keywords for better searchability.

Example :

"Glamour Cosmetics Ltd. is dedicated to creating high-quality, cruelty-free beauty products. Our mission is to empower individuals to express their unique beauty with confidence. We pride ourselves on innovation, sustainability, and customer satisfaction."

6. Add Specialties and Contact Details

Specialties : List your company's specialties to highlight your areas of expertise. This helps visitors understand what your business excels at.

Contact Information : Provide contact details, including a company email and phone number, to facilitate communication with potential clients and partners.

Example :

"Specialties : Skincare, Makeup, Organic Beauty Products. Contact us at info@glamourcosmetics.com or call (123) 456-7890."

7. Publish Your Company Page

Review : Double-check all the information for accuracy and completeness. Once satisfied, click the "Create Page" button to publish your company page.

Example :

"Review your company details and click 'Create Page' to make your LinkedIn company page live."

Showcasing Your Business : How to Highlight Your Business Achievements

After setting up your LinkedIn company page, it's essential to continuously update and showcase your business achievements to keep your audience engaged and attract new followers. Here's how to effectively highlight your business achievements :

Why Showcasing Achievements Matters

1. Credibility : Demonstrates your company's successes and builds trust with your audience.

2. Engagement : Keeps your audience informed and engaged with your latest milestones and innovations.

3. Attraction : Attracts potential clients, partners, and top talent by showcasing your accomplishments.

Strategies for Highlighting Business Achievements

1. Share Company Updates and Milestones

Regular Posts : Share updates about significant milestones, such as new product launches, partnerships, awards, and company growth. Use engaging visuals and compelling copy to capture attention.

Example :

"Excited to announce that Glamour Cosmetics Ltd. has just launched our new organic skincare line! This innovative collection is designed to nourish and rejuvenate your skin naturally. #BeautyInnovation #OrganicSkincare"

2. Publish Success Stories and Case Studies

Detailed Case Studies : Publish detailed case studies that highlight how your products or services have helped clients achieve their goals. Include metrics and testimonials to add credibility.

Example :

"Check out our latest case study on how our eco-friendly packaging solutions helped XYZ Shoe Outlet reduce their carbon footprint by 40%. Read the full story here : [link] #Sustainability #EcoFriendly"

3. Highlight Employee Achievements

Employee Spotlights : Showcase the achievements of your employees to highlight your company culture and the talent within your organization. Celebrate promotions, project successes, and awards.

Example :

"Congratulations to our lead designer, Jane Doe, for receiving the 'Innovator of the Year' award! Her dedication and creativity have been instrumental in our recent product developments. #EmployeeSpotlight #TeamSuccess"

4. Share Industry Insights and Thought Leadership

Thought Leadership : Publish articles and posts that share your company's insights and expertise on industry trends and best practices. Position your company as a thought leader in your field.

Example :

"Discover the latest trends in sustainable furniture design and how our innovative techniques are setting new standards in the industry. Read our latest article by our CEO, John Smith : [link] #FurnitureDesign #Sustainability"

5. Engage with Multimedia Content

Visual Content : Use high-quality images, infographics, videos, and presentations to showcase your achievements. Multimedia content is more engaging and can help convey complex information more effectively.

Example :

"Watch our latest video to see how our taxi app, GoRide, is revolutionizing urban transportation with real-time tracking and seamless payment options. [link] #TechInnovation #UrbanMobility"

6. Encourage Client and Partner Testimonials

Testimonials : Share testimonials from satisfied clients and partners to build trust and demonstrate the value of your offerings. Highlight specific benefits and outcomes.

Example :

"We're thrilled to share this testimonial from our client, ABC Franchise, who achieved a 50% increase in sales with our comprehensive marketing strategy. 'Partnering with XYZ Marketing has been a game-changer for our business!' #ClientTestimonials #BusinessGrowth"

Examples of Effective Business Profiles : Analysis of Successful LinkedIn Business Pages

Analyzing successful LinkedIn business pages can provide valuable insights into what makes them effective. Here are examples of well-optimized business profiles from different industries, highlighting their strengths and best practices :

Example 1 : Cosmetics Manufacturing

Company : Glamour Cosmetics Ltd.

Key Elements :

- Compelling Banner and Logo : High-quality visuals that reflect the brand's identity.

- Engaging Description : Clear and concise company overview that highlights the mission, values, and unique selling points.

- Regular Updates : Frequent posts about product launches, industry insights, and company news.

- Showcased Specialties : Listed specialties such as Skincare, Makeup, and Organic Beauty Products.

- Client Testimonials : Featured testimonials from satisfied clients.

Outcome : High engagement from followers, strong brand presence, and successful talent acquisition.

Example 2 : Shoe Outlets

Company : SoleMates Shoe Outlets

Key Elements :

- Professional Branding : Clean and professional logo and banner image.

- Detailed Description : Comprehensive company description that outlines services, target market, and commitment to customer satisfaction.

- Success Stories : Regularly shared success stories and case studies that demonstrate the impact of their services.

- Employee Spotlights : Highlighted employee achievements and contributions to foster a positive company culture.

- Industry Leadership : Published articles on footwear trends and best practices.

Outcome : Enhanced credibility in the footwear industry, increased client inquiries, and strong employee engagement.

Example 3 : Furniture Manufacturing

Company : Comfort Furniture Co.

Key Elements :

- Vibrant Branding : Eye-catching logo and banner that convey creativity and innovation.

- Engaging Content : Frequent updates with a mix of industry insights, client success stories, and company achievements.

- Visual Content : Utilized videos, infographics, and images to showcase their work and results.

- Client Testimonials : Featured glowing testimonials from high-profile clients.

- Employee Recognition : Highlighted team achievements and company culture through employee spotlights.

Outcome : High follower engagement, increased client interest, and strong brand reputation.

Example 4 : Branded Franchisees

Company : FastFood Franchise Inc.

Key Elements :

- Professional Branding : Clean and professional logo and banner image.

- Detailed Description : Comprehensive company description that outlines services, target market, and commitment to quality and consistency.

- Success Stories : Regularly shared success stories and case studies that demonstrate the impact of their franchise model.

- Employee Spotlights : Highlighted employee achievements and contributions to foster a positive company culture.

- Industry Leadership : Published articles on franchise management and best practices.

Outcome : Enhanced credibility in the franchise industry, increased client inquiries, and strong employee engagement.

Example 5 : Taxi App

Company : GoRide Taxi Services

Key Elements :

- Vibrant Branding

 : Eye-catching logo and banner that convey innovation and reliability.

- Engaging Content : Frequent updates with a mix of industry insights, client success stories, and company achievements.

- Visual Content : Utilized videos, infographics, and images to showcase their services and technological innovations.

- Client Testimonials : Featured glowing testimonials from satisfied users.

- Employee Recognition : Highlighted team achievements and company culture through employee spotlights.

Outcome : High follower engagement, increased client interest, and strong brand reputation.

Leveraging ChatGPT to Promote Your Business on LinkedIn

Using AI tools like ChatGPT can significantly enhance your LinkedIn marketing efforts by generating creative content, engaging posts, and personalized messages. Here's how to leverage ChatGPT to promote your business on LinkedIn :

Why Use ChatGPT for LinkedIn Promotion

1. Content Generation : Quickly create engaging and relevant content to keep your audience informed and entertained.

2. Efficiency : Save time by automating the creation of posts, articles, and messages.

3. Personalization : Generate personalized messages and responses to engage with your audience effectively.

Strategies for Using ChatGPT

1. Create Engaging Posts

Prompt : "Generate a LinkedIn post announcing our new product launch, highlighting its features and benefits."

Output :

"We're excited to introduce our latest product, the Eco-Friendly Sofa Collection! Designed to combine style and sustainability, our new collection offers comfort without compromising on environmental responsibility. Discover how our innovative designs can enhance your living space. Learn more : [link] #SustainableLiving #FurnitureDesign"

2. Write Compelling Articles

Prompt : "Write a LinkedIn article on the top 5 trends in digital marketing for 2024."

Output :

"Stay Ahead of the Curve : Top 5 Digital Marketing Trends for 2024

As we move into 2024, the digital marketing landscape continues to evolve rapidly. Here are the top 5 trends that every marketer should watch :

1. AI and Machine Learning : Leveraging AI to deliver personalized experiences and optimize campaigns.

2. Voice Search Optimization : Ensuring your content is voice-search friendly as more users adopt smart speakers.

3. Video Marketing : Creating engaging video content to capture audience attention and drive conversions.

4. Influencer Marketing : Partnering with influencers to reach new audiences and build brand credibility.

5. Data Privacy : Navigating new regulations and building trust through transparent data practices.

Read more : [link] #DigitalMarketing #MarketingTrends #2024"

3. Generate Personalized Messages

Prompt : "Create a personalized message to invite a potential client to a demo of our software solution."

Output :

"Hi [Name],

I hope this message finds you well. I'm reaching out to introduce you to our AI-Powered Analytics Platform, designed to provide real-time insights and predictive analytics tailored to your business needs. I would love to offer you a personalized demo to showcase how our solution can drive your business success. Are you available for a demo next week?

Looking forward to your response.

Best regards,

[Your Name]"

4. Respond to Comments and Messages

Prompt : "Generate a response to a client's positive feedback on our recent product launch post."

Output :

"Hi [Name],

Thank you so much for your kind words! We're thrilled to hear that you're excited about our new Eco-Friendly Sofa Collection. Our team has worked hard to create a solution that meets the needs of environmentally conscious consumers. If you have any questions or would like to learn more, feel free to reach out. We appreciate your support!

Best regards,
[Your Name]"

Conclusion

LinkedIn provides entrepreneurs and business owners with a powerful platform to establish their brand presence, showcase their achievements, and engage with their audience. By following a structured approach to creating a company page, highlighting business achievements, analyzing successful profiles, and leveraging AI tools like ChatGPT, you can effectively promote your business and achieve your professional goals. Implement these strategies to maximize your LinkedIn impact and drive business growth.

Chapter 11

ADVANCED LINKEDIN STRATEGIES

Content Creation and Sharing : How to Create and Share Valuable Content

Creating and sharing valuable content on LinkedIn is essential for establishing thought leadership, engaging your audience, and driving meaningful interactions. Here's how to craft compelling content and share it effectively :

Why Content Creation Matters

1. Engagement : High-quality content encourages engagement, fosters conversations, and builds relationships with your audience.

2. Credibility : Consistently sharing valuable content positions you as a thought leader in your industry.

3. Visibility : Regular content updates keep you visible in your network's feed, increasing your reach and influence.

Strategies for Effective Content Creation

1. Identify Your Audience

Understand Your Audience : Know who your target audience is, including their interests, challenges, and what type of content they find valuable. This helps tailor your content to meet their needs.

Example :

"If you're targeting marketing professionals, focus on sharing insights about digital marketing trends, best practices, and case studies."

2. Create Valuable Content

Types of Content : Share a mix of content types, including articles, videos, infographics, and slide decks. Each format caters to different preferences and keeps your content diverse and engaging.

Example :

"Write an article on 'Top 5 Digital Marketing Trends for 2024,' create a video tutorial on 'Using SEO to Boost Your Website Traffic,' and design an infographic summarizing 'Key Metrics for Marketing Success.'"

Provide Insights : Offer actionable insights, tips, and expertise that your audience can apply. Avoid overly promotional content; focus on delivering value.

Example :

"Share a post with actionable tips on 'How to Optimize Your LinkedIn Profile for Job Searches' and include specific steps and examples."

3. Maintain a Consistent Posting Schedule

Regular Updates : Consistency is key. Develop a content calendar and stick to a regular posting schedule to keep your audience engaged and anticipate your updates.

Example :

"Post twice a week, sharing a mix of articles, industry news, and success stories. Schedule posts for Tuesday and Thursday mornings when engagement rates are typically higher."

4. Engage with Your Audience

Interactive Content : Encourage interactions by asking questions, hosting polls, and inviting feedback. Respond to comments and messages to foster a sense of community.

Example :

"Post a poll asking your audience 'What's the biggest challenge you face in digital marketing?' and follow up with a discussion based on the results."

5. Leverage Hashtags and Mentions

Relevant Hashtags : Use relevant hashtags to increase the discoverability of your content. Mention industry influencers and companies to expand your reach and engage with a broader audience.

Example :

"Include hashtags like #DigitalMarketing, #SEO, and #ContentStrategy in your posts. Mention industry leaders like @MarketingProfs and @NeilPatel to boost visibility."

Best Practices for Sharing Content

1. Optimize for LinkedIn

Native Content : Share content directly on LinkedIn rather than just linking to external sources. Native content tends to perform better in terms of engagement.

Example :

"Publish an article directly on LinkedIn Pulse rather than linking to an external blog. Share native videos and slide decks using LinkedIn's upload features."

2. Use Compelling Visuals

Visual Appeal : Accompany your posts with high-quality images, graphics, and videos. Visual content is more engaging and can significantly increase interaction rates.

Example :

"Share a visually appealing infographic summarizing '10 Ways to Improve Your LinkedIn Profile,' complete with statistics and tips."

3. Craft Attention-Grabbing Headlines

Engaging Headlines : Write headlines that capture attention and encourage clicks. Use clear, concise language and include keywords relevant to your audience's interests.

Example :

"'Unlock the Secrets to LinkedIn Success : 5 Proven Strategies' is more engaging than 'LinkedIn Tips.'"

Using LinkedIn Analytics : How to Use Analytics to Improve Your Profile

LinkedIn Analytics provides valuable insights into how your content and profile are performing. By understanding and leveraging these analytics, you can refine your strategy and improve your LinkedIn presence.

Why LinkedIn Analytics Matter

1. Performance Measurement : Track the success of your content and profile, identifying what works and what doesn't.

2. Audience Insights : Gain insights into your audience's demographics, interests, and engagement patterns.

3. Optimization : Use data-driven insights to optimize your content strategy and profile for better results.

Key LinkedIn Analytics Features

1. Profile Views

Who's Viewing Your Profile : See who has viewed your profile, including their industry, job title, and company. This helps identify potential leads and connections.

Example :

"Notice a spike in profile views from marketing managers. Consider reaching out to these viewers to build connections."

2. Post and Article Performance

Engagement Metrics : Analyze likes, comments, shares, and views for your posts and articles. Identify which types of content resonate most with your audience.

Example :

"An article on 'Digital Marketing Trends' received high engagement. Plan to create more content on similar topics."

3. Follower Demographics

Audience Breakdown : View demographic information about your followers, such as their industry, job function, and location. Tailor your content to better match their interests.

Example :

"Most followers are from the tech industry. Focus on creating tech-related content to engage this audience."

4. Company Page Insights

Page Analytics : For company pages, track follower growth, post engagement, and visitor metrics. Understand how your page is performing and where improvements can be made.

Example :

"Visitor metrics show high traffic on Mondays. Schedule important updates and announcements for early in the week."

Strategies for Using LinkedIn Analytics

1. Regular Monitoring

Consistent Tracking : Regularly check your analytics to stay updated on your profile and content performance. Adjust your strategy based on the latest data.

Example :

"Review your LinkedIn Analytics dashboard weekly to track progress and identify trends."

2. Set Goals and KPIs

Clear Objectives : Define clear goals and key performance indicators (KPIs) for your LinkedIn activities, such as increasing profile views, growing your follower base, or boosting post engagement.

Example :

"Set a goal to increase profile views by 20% in the next quarter. Track progress using profile view analytics."

3. Experiment and Optimize

A/B Testing : Experiment with different types of content, posting times, and engagement strategies. Use analytics to determine what works best and optimize accordingly.

Example :

"Test posting articles in the morning versus the afternoon. Use engagement metrics to identify the optimal posting time."

4. Leverage Audience Insights

Targeted Content : Use audience demographics to create content that resonates with your followers. Address their specific interests and pain points.

Example :

"If most followers are in marketing, create content focused on marketing strategies, tools, and case studies."

LinkedIn Advertising : Overview of Advertising Options and Strategies

LinkedIn advertising offers various options to help you reach a broader audience, generate leads, and promote your brand. Here's an overview of LinkedIn's advertising options and strategies for leveraging them effectively :

Why LinkedIn Advertising Matters

1. Targeted Reach : Reach a highly targeted audience based on professional criteria such as job title, industry, and company size.

2. Lead Generation : Generate high-quality leads through tailored ad campaigns.

3. Brand Awareness : Increase brand visibility and awareness among professionals in your industry.

LinkedIn Advertising Options

1. Sponsored Content

Native Ads : Promote your content directly in the LinkedIn feed. Sponsored Content appears as native posts, blending seamlessly with organic content.

Example :

"Promote a thought leadership article on 'The Future of AI in Business' to reach decision-makers in the tech industry."

2. Sponsored InMail

Direct Messaging : Send personalized messages directly to LinkedIn members' inboxes. Sponsored InMail is ideal for targeted promotions and event invitations.

Example :

"Send an exclusive invite to a webinar on 'Advanced Digital Marketing Strategies' to marketing directors and CMOs."

3. Text Ads

Simple Ads : Display text-based ads in the sidebar of LinkedIn pages. Text Ads are cost-effective and can drive traffic to your website or LinkedIn page.

Example :

"Run a Text Ad campaign promoting a free eBook on 'Effective Project Management Techniques' to project managers."

4. Dynamic Ads

Personalized Ads : Use Dynamic Ads to create personalized ad experiences. These ads automatically customize based on the viewer's profile information.

Example :

"Create a Dynamic Ad campaign offering personalized job recommendations for software developers based on their LinkedIn profiles."

5. Video Ads

Engaging Content : Use video ads to deliver engaging, multimedia content directly in the LinkedIn feed. Video ads are effective for storytelling and showcasing products or services.

Example :

"Launch a video ad campaign highlighting your company's latest product features and customer testimonials."

Strategies for Effective LinkedIn Advertising

1. Define Your Objectives

Clear Goals : Set clear objectives for your LinkedIn ad campaigns, such as brand awareness, lead generation, or event promotion. Define KPIs to measure success.

Example :

"Objective : Generate 100 new leads for a product demo. KPI : Number of leads captured through the campaign."

2. Target the Right Audience

Detailed Targeting : Use LinkedIn's targeting options to reach your ideal audience. Narrow down your audience based on job title, industry, company size, and other relevant criteria.

Example :

"Target decision-makers in the finance industry with job titles such as CFO, Finance Director, and Financial Analyst."

3. Craft Compelling Ad Copy and Visuals

Engaging Content : Write clear, compelling ad copy that highlights the benefits of your offering. Use high-quality visuals or videos to capture attention.

Example :

"Ad Copy : 'Unlock the Power of AI for Your Business. Join our exclusive webinar and learn how to leverage AI for growth.' Visual : Eye-catching image of a business professional using AI technology."

4. Monitor and Optimize Campaigns

Performance Tracking : Regularly monitor your ad performance using LinkedIn's campaign manager. Adjust your targeting, ad copy, and budget based on performance data.

Example :

"Monitor click-through rates (CTR) and conversion rates. If a particular ad isn't performing well, tweak the copy or imagery and re-test."

5. Leverage LinkedIn Analytics

Data-Driven Insights : Use LinkedIn Analytics to gain insights into your ad performance and audience engagement. Use this data to refine your advertising strategy.

Example :

"Analyze which ad variations are driving the most conversions. Use these insights to create more effective future campaigns."

Conclusion

Advanced LinkedIn strategies, such as content creation and sharing, leveraging LinkedIn Analytics, and utilizing LinkedIn advertising, can significantly enhance your presence on the platform. By consistently creating valuable content, using analytics to refine your approach, and strategically implementing LinkedIn advertising, you can achieve your professional and business goals. Implement these strategies to maximize your LinkedIn impact and drive meaningful results.

Chapter 12

MAINTAINING YOUR LINKEDIN PROFILE

Regular Updates : Importance of Keeping Your Profile Current

Your LinkedIn profile is a dynamic representation of your professional journey. Regular updates ensure it remains relevant, accurate, and engaging, helping you to attract opportunities, showcase your growth, and stay connected with your network.

Why Regular Updates Matter

1. Reflects Current Skills and Experience : An updated profile accurately represents your latest skills, experiences, and accomplishments, making it easier for recruiters and connections to understand your professional value.

2. Enhances Visibility : Regular updates can increase your profile's visibility in search results and keep you top-of-mind within your network.

3. Demonstrates Active Engagement : A frequently updated profile shows that you are actively engaged in your professional development and the LinkedIn community.

Strategies for Regular Updates

1. Update Work Experience and Skills

New Roles and Projects : Whenever you take on a new role, complete a significant project, or learn a new skill, update your profile to reflect these changes.

Example :

"Add your latest promotion to Senior Marketing Manager and detail your role in launching a successful rebranding campaign."

2. Refresh Your Profile Picture and Banner

Professional Photos : Use a recent, high-quality photo that reflects your current appearance and professional image. Update your banner to align with your latest achievements or company branding.

Example :

"Replace your old profile picture with a new, professionally-taken headshot. Update your banner to feature a recent industry award you received."

3. Revise Your Summary and Headline

Current Focus : Ensure your summary and headline reflect your current professional focus, goals, and the value you bring to your field.

Example :

"Revise your headline to 'Experienced Product Manager | Agile Methodologies | Driving Innovation in Tech' and update your summary to highlight recent achievements and future aspirations."

4. Add New Certifications and Education

Continued Learning : Highlight any new certifications, courses, or educational achievements to showcase your commitment to continuous learning and professional growth.

Example :

"Add your recent certification in Data Science from Coursera and update your education section to include your latest workshop on Leadership Skills."

5. Regularly Share Content

Stay Active : Post articles, share industry news, and comment on updates to stay active and engaged with your network. Regular activity keeps your profile visible and relevant.

Example :

"Share a recent article you wrote on emerging trends in artificial intelligence and engage with comments to spark discussion."

Engaging with Your Network : Strategies for Ongoing Engagement

Maintaining an active and engaged network on LinkedIn requires consistent interaction and meaningful engagement. Here are strategies to keep your network vibrant and engaged :

Why Ongoing Engagement Matters

1. Strengthens Relationships : Regular engagement helps maintain and strengthen professional relationships, fostering a supportive and connected network.

2. Increases Visibility : Active participation increases your visibility within your network, leading to more opportunities and interactions.

3. Builds Credibility : Sharing insights and engaging in discussions positions you as a thought leader in your field.

Strategies for Engaging with Your Network

1. Consistently Share Valuable Content

Relevant Posts : Share articles, industry news, and insights that are relevant to your network's interests. Provide your own commentary to add value.

Example :

"Post an article on the latest developments in renewable energy, adding your insights on how these changes will impact the industry."

2. Participate in Group Discussions

Active Participation : Join LinkedIn groups related to your industry and actively participate in discussions. Share your expertise and engage with other members' posts.

Example :

"Join the 'Digital Marketing Professionals' group and contribute to a discussion on effective SEO strategies by sharing your experiences and tips."

3. Comment and React to Posts

Meaningful Engagement : Regularly comment on and react to posts from your connections. Meaningful interactions show that you value their content and foster deeper connections.

Example :

"Comment on a connection's post about their recent project success, offering congratulations and asking insightful questions about their approach."

4. Send Personalized Messages

Stay Connected : Periodically send personalized messages to your connections to check in, congratulate them on their achievements, or share relevant opportunities.

Example :

"Send a message to a former colleague congratulating them on their recent promotion and suggesting a virtual coffee catch-up."

5. Celebrate Milestones and Achievements

Acknowledge Successes : Celebrate your connections' professional milestones, such as promotions, work anniversaries, and new jobs. This strengthens relationships and shows you care.

Example :

"Congratulate a connection on their work anniversary with a personalized message acknowledging their contributions and growth."

Monitoring Your Profile's Performance : Tools and Tips for Tracking Success

Regularly monitoring your LinkedIn profile's performance helps you understand what's working and where improvements are needed. Use LinkedIn's analytics tools to gain insights and refine your strategy.

Why Monitoring Performance Matters

1. **Understand Impact** : Analytics help you measure the effectiveness of your LinkedIn activities and understand how well your profile is performing.

2. **Identify Opportunities :** Performance data reveals opportunities for improvement and areas where you can focus your efforts.

3. **Optimize Strategy :** Continuous monitoring allows you to adjust your strategy based on what's resonating with your audience.

Tools and Tips for Monitoring Performance

1. LinkedIn Profile Views

Track Views : Regularly check who's viewing your profile to gain insights into the types of professionals interested in your profile. Use this information to tailor your content and networking efforts.

Example :

"Notice an increase in profile views from marketing professionals. Consider sharing more marketing-related content to engage this audience."

2. Post and Article Analytics

Engagement Metrics : Analyze likes, comments, shares, and views for your posts and articles. Identify which types of content perform best and why.

Example :

"Review analytics for your latest article on 'Remote Work Productivity Tips' and note the high engagement. Plan more content on similar topics."

3. Follower Demographics

Audience Insights : Use LinkedIn's analytics to understand your followers' demographics, such as their industries, job functions, and locations. Tailor your content to better meet their interests.

Example :

"Analyze follower demographics to find a large portion are in the tech industry. Focus on creating content related to technology trends and innovations."

4. Company Page Insights

Performance Tracking : For those managing LinkedIn company pages, track metrics such as visitor metrics, follower growth, and engagement rates. Use these insights to optimize your company's LinkedIn presence.

Example :

"Monitor your company page's follower growth and post

engagement to understand which types of updates drive the most interaction."

5. Use Third-Party Tools

Advanced Analytics : Consider using third-party analytics tools for more detailed insights and advanced tracking capabilities. Tools like Hootsuite, Sprout Social, or LinkedIn's own Sales Navigator can provide deeper analysis.

Example :

"Use Hootsuite to schedule LinkedIn posts and track engagement metrics over time, comparing the performance of different content types."

6. Set Performance Goals

Define Metrics : Set clear performance goals and key metrics to track, such as increasing profile views, boosting post engagement, or growing your network.

Example :

"Set a goal to increase your post engagement rate by 20% over the next quarter. Monitor progress using LinkedIn's engagement analytics."

Conclusion

Maintaining your LinkedIn profile involves regular updates, consistent engagement with your network, and continuous monitoring of your profile's performance. By keeping your profile current, actively interacting with your connections, and leveraging analytics tools, you can maximize your LinkedIn presence and achieve your professional goals. Implement these strategies to ensure your LinkedIn profile remains dynamic, relevant, and impactful.

Chapter 13

LINKEDIN PROFILE PICTURE AND BANNER

Choosing the Correct Profile Picture : Standard Rules and Strategies

Your LinkedIn profile picture is often the first impression you make on potential connections, recruiters, and clients. A professional and approachable image can significantly enhance your profile's appeal. Here are some standard rules and strategies to choose the correct profile picture :

Why Your Profile Picture Matters

1. First Impressions : It's the first visual element people see and can influence their perception of you.

2. Professionalism : A high-quality photo conveys professionalism and credibility.

3. Personal Connection : An approachable picture helps in making a personal connection with your audience.

Standard Rules for a Professional Profile Picture

1. High-Quality Image

Clear and Crisp : Use a high-resolution image that is clear and sharp. Avoid blurry or pixelated photos.

Example :

"A well-lit headshot taken with a high-resolution camera ensures clarity and sharpness."

2. Appropriate Attire

Dress Professionally : Wear attire that is appropriate for your industry. For corporate roles, a suit or business casual attire is suitable. For creative fields, more relaxed attire may be acceptable.

Example :

"For a corporate finance role, wear a suit and tie. For a graphic design position, a stylish but professional outfit works well."

3. Neutral Background

Avoid Distractions : Use a simple, uncluttered background that keeps the focus on you. Neutral colors like white, gray, or a soft blur are ideal.

Example :

"Choose a plain white or light gray background, or use a professional backdrop with a subtle gradient."

4. Friendly Expression

Smile Naturally : A genuine smile makes you appear approachable and friendly. Avoid overly serious or stern expressions.

Example :

"A natural, friendly smile with a slight tilt of the head can make a positive impression."

5. Proper Lighting

Well-Lit : Ensure your face is well-lit, with no harsh shadows.

Natural light is often the best, but soft, diffused artificial lighting can also work.

Example :

"Position yourself facing a window with natural light, or use a ring light to ensure even lighting."

Strategies for Choosing the Correct Profile Picture

1. Professional Photography

Invest in a Pro : If possible, invest in a professional headshot. A professional photographer can ensure optimal lighting, background, and composition.

Example :

"Hire a professional photographer for a headshot session, ensuring you receive a polished and high-quality image."

2. DIY with Care

Self-Taken Photos : If a professional shoot isn't possible, use a high-quality camera or smartphone, a tripod, and proper lighting to take your own photo.

Example :

"Use your smartphone's portrait mode, a tripod, and natural lighting from a window to take a professional-looking headshot."

3. Consistent Branding

Uniformity : Ensure your LinkedIn profile picture aligns with other professional photos you use on social media, your website, and business cards for consistent personal branding.

Example :

"Use the same headshot across LinkedIn, Twitter, and your professional website to maintain a consistent personal brand."

Choosing the Correct Banner Image : Standard Rules and Strategies

The banner image on your LinkedIn profile is a powerful tool to enhance your personal brand and make your profile stand out. Here are standard rules and strategies to choose the correct banner image :

Why Your Banner Image Matters

1. Visual Appeal : Adds visual interest and personality to your profile.

2. Branding Opportunity : Serves as a canvas to showcase your personal or business brand.

3. Professional Context : Provides context about your profession, industry, or interests.

Standard Rules for a Professional Banner Image

1. High Resolution

Quality Matters : Use a high-resolution image that looks good on all devices. A pixelated or blurry banner can detract from your profile's professionalism.

Example :

"Choose an image with a resolution of at least 1584 x 396 pixels to ensure it displays well on different screen sizes."

2. Relevant to Your Profession

Industry Context : Select an image that relates to your industry or profession. It should give visitors a sense of what you do or what your business represents.

Example :

"For a tech professional, a banner featuring abstract technology patterns or a city skyline could be relevant. For a healthcare worker, an image of a healthcare facility or medical symbols would be appropriate."

3. Brand Colors

Consistency : Use colors that match your personal or company brand to create a cohesive look. This consistency strengthens your visual identity.

Example :

"If your brand colors are blue and white, incorporate these colors into your banner image to align with your overall branding."

4. Clean and Uncluttered

Focus on Simplicity : Avoid overly busy or cluttered images. The banner should complement your profile without overwhelming it.

Example :

"Choose a simple image with a clear focal point, like a skyline with ample sky space or a minimalist office setup."

Strategies for Choosing the Correct Banner Image

1. Showcase Your Work

Portfolio Highlight : Use the banner to showcase a sample of your work, especially if you're in a creative field. This could include a collage of your best projects or a high-quality image of a recent project.

Example :

"A graphic designer could use a banner featuring a montage of their designs. A writer could display a banner with a cover image of their latest publication."

2. Incorporate Text Wisely

Subtle Text : If you include text, make sure it's minimal and relevant, such as a tagline or your company's mission statement.

Ensure the text is readable and doesn't overshadow the image.

Example :

"Add your company's tagline in a clean, readable font on one side of the banner, leaving the rest of the image uncluttered."

3. Seasonal and Timely Updates

Stay Current : Update your banner image to reflect current projects, seasons, or events. This keeps your profile looking fresh and relevant.

Example :

"Change your banner to feature holiday themes during the festive season or showcase a major event your company is hosting."

Leveraging AI Tools like DALL-E and MidJourney to Generate Images for Banners

Artificial Intelligence (AI) tools like DALL-E and MidJourney can help you create unique and professional banner images tailored to your brand. Here's how to leverage these AI tools effectively :

Why Use AI Tools for Banner Images

1. Customization : AI tools allow you to create highly customized images that perfectly fit your brand's aesthetic.

2. Innovation : Generate unique, eye-catching designs that stand out from standard stock images.

3. Efficiency : Quickly produce high-quality images without needing extensive design skills or software.

Strategies for Using AI Tools

1. DALL-E : Creative Image Generation

AI Creativity : DALL-E, developed by OpenAI, uses AI to generate images from textual descriptions. This allows for highly creative and customized visuals.

Example :

"Input a description like 'A futuristic city skyline at sunset with holographic advertisements' to generate a unique and visually appealing banner for a tech company."

How to Use :

- Define Your Needs : Clearly describe the image you want in detail.

- Input Description : Enter the description into DALL-E and generate several image options.

- Refine and Select : Choose the best image and make any necessary refinements using photo editing tools.

2. MidJourney : Artistic Image Creation

Artistic Flair : MidJourney specializes in creating artistic and visually stunning images. Use it to generate banner images that have a unique, hand-crafted feel.

Example :

"Generate a banner with a description like 'A serene mountain landscape in watercolor style' to create a calming and professional backdrop for a wellness coach's profile."

How to Use :

- Join the Community : MidJourney operates through a Discord community where you can input image prompts.

- Input Prompt : Provide a detailed prompt describing your desired image.

- Select and Download : Review the generated images, select the one that fits best, and download it for use as your banner.

Tips for Effective AI-Generated Banners

1. Clear Descriptions

Be Specific : The more specific and detailed your description, the better the AI can generate a suitable image.

Example :

"Instead of 'office setup,' use 'modern office setup with a wooden desk, laptop, and a plant in a minimalist style.'"

2. Experiment with Variations

Multiple Iterations : Generate multiple variations of your description to find the best fit. AI tools can create several options from the same prompt.

Example :

"Generate different versions of 'city skyline at night with neon lights' to choose the most visually appealing one."

3. Edit and Refine

Final Touches : Use photo editing software to make final adjustments to the AI-generated images, ensuring they perfectly match your profile's look and feel.

Example :

"Adjust the brightness, contrast, and cropping of the AI-generated image to ensure it fits well within LinkedIn's banner dimensions."

Conclusion

Choosing the correct profile picture and banner image for your LinkedIn profile is crucial for making a strong and professional impression. By following standard rules and strategies, and leveraging advanced AI tools like DALL-E and MidJourney, you can create visually appealing and unique images that enhance your personal brand. Regularly updating and customizing these visual elements will keep your profile fresh, engaging, and reflective of your professional journey. Implement these strategies to make your LinkedIn profile stand out and leave a lasting impression.

Chapter 14

CASE STUDIES AND SUCCESS STORIES

Profiles of Key Personalities : Detailed Look at How Influential People Use LinkedIn

LinkedIn is a powerful platform utilized by influential people across various industries to build their brands, connect with their audience, and drive their professional goals. By examining the profiles and strategies of key personalities, we can uncover valuable insights into effective LinkedIn usage.

Why Studying Influential Profiles Matters

1. Inspiration : Provides inspiration and practical ideas for enhancing your own LinkedIn presence.

2. Best Practices : Highlights effective strategies that can be adapted to different contexts and goals.

3. Success Patterns : Identifies common patterns and tactics that contribute to LinkedIn success.

Key Personalities on LinkedIn

1. Satya Nadella, CEO of Microsoft

Profile Overview : Satya Nadella's LinkedIn profile is a masterclass in executive branding. His profile features a professional headshot, a compelling headline, and a detailed summary that outlines his vision for Microsoft and his commitment to innovation.

Strategies :

- Thought Leadership : Nadella regularly shares articles, insights, and updates about Microsoft's initiatives, industry trends, and his personal reflections on leadership and technology.

- Engagement : He actively engages with his network by liking, commenting on, and sharing content that aligns with his professional interests.

- Company Advocacy : Nadella uses his profile to advocate for Microsoft's values, culture, and products, reinforcing the company's brand through his personal brand.

Example Post :

"Excited to share our latest advancements in AI and how they are transforming industries. At Microsoft, we are committed to empowering every person and organization on the planet to achieve more. #AI #Innovation #TechLeadership"

2. Arianna Huffington, Founder of Thrive Global

Profile Overview : Arianna Huffington's profile emphasizes her role as a thought leader in wellness and productivity. Her summary highlights her mission to end the stress and burnout epidemic, and her posts reflect her passion for fostering healthier work environments.

Strategies :

- Personal Branding : Huffington's profile is consistently branded with her message of wellness and productivity. Her posts often include personal anecdotes and motivational quotes.

- Content Sharing : She frequently shares content from Thrive Global, including articles, videos, and success stories that resonate with her audience.

- Network Engagement : Huffington engages with her network through interactive posts, asking questions and encouraging discussions around wellness topics.

Example Post :

"Taking time to recharge is essential for productivity and creativity. How do you prioritize self-care in your daily routine? #Wellness #SelfCare #Productivity"

3. Gary Vaynerchuk, CEO of VaynerMedia

Profile Overview : Gary Vaynerchuk's LinkedIn profile is energetic and motivational, reflecting his dynamic personality and entrepreneurial spirit. His content focuses on business advice, personal development, and digital marketing trends.

Strategies :

- Video Content : Vaynerchuk leverages video content extensively, sharing daily videos that offer practical business tips and motivational messages.

- Authenticity : His posts are characterized by a high level of authenticity and transparency, often sharing his personal experiences and lessons learned.

- Engagement : Vaynerchuk actively responds to comments and engages in discussions, fostering a strong sense of community among his followers.

Example Post :

"Patience and hard work are the keys to success. It's about putting in the effort every single day and playing the long game. How do you stay motivated? #Entrepreneurship #Motivation #Hustle"

Industry-Specific Examples : Tailored Advice for Different Sectors

Different industries have unique characteristics and demands, and effective LinkedIn strategies can vary accordingly. Here's tailored advice for using LinkedIn in specific sectors :

Technology

Key Strategies :

- Highlight Innovation : Showcase your involvement in cutting-edge projects, technological advancements, and innovative solutions.

- Engage with Tech Communities : Join and participate in LinkedIn groups related to technology, software development, and innovation.

- Share Technical Content : Regularly post technical articles, how-to guides, and case studies that demonstrate your expertise.

Example :

"A software engineer can share a detailed post about a recent project involving machine learning, including the challenges faced and the solutions implemented. Engaging with other engineers in relevant LinkedIn groups can also provide valuable networking opportunities."

Finance

Key Strategies :

- Demonstrate Expertise : Share insights on financial trends, market analysis, and investment strategies to establish credibility.

- Network with Industry Leaders : Connect with finance professionals, attend virtual conferences, and participate in discussions on economic issues.

- Highlight Credentials : Clearly showcase certifications, professional achievements, and educational background.

Example :

"A financial analyst can post an in-depth analysis of the current economic climate, including data visualizations and predictions. Connecting with other analysts and joining finance-related groups can enhance professional visibility."

Healthcare

Key Strategies :

- Share Knowledge : Post articles and updates about medical research, healthcare innovations, and patient care best practices.

- Engage with Healthcare Communities : Join groups and engage in discussions with other healthcare professionals to share knowledge and experiences.

- Showcase Impact : Highlight contributions to patient care, public health initiatives, and community service.

Example :

"A nurse can share stories about patient care innovations implemented at their hospital, including the outcomes and benefits. Participating in healthcare groups and forums on LinkedIn can also help in building a professional network."

Lessons Learned : Key Takeaways from Successful LinkedIn Users

Studying successful LinkedIn users provides valuable lessons that can be applied to enhance your own profile and strategy. Here are key takeaways from influential LinkedIn personalities :

Key Takeaways

1. Consistency is Key

Regular Updates : Consistently update your profile and share content to keep your network engaged and your profile visible.

Example :

"Successful users like Gary Vaynerchuk post daily, ensuring their content remains fresh and their audience engaged."

2. Authenticity Matters

Be Genuine : Authenticity fosters trust and connection. Share personal stories, lessons learned, and honest insights.

Example :

"Arianna Huffington's posts often include personal anecdotes and reflections, making her content relatable and engaging."

3. Engage Actively

Interaction : Actively engage with your network by commenting on posts, responding to messages, and participating in discussions.

Example :

"Satya Nadella frequently engages with posts about Microsoft's initiatives, sparking conversations and building community."

4. Showcase Expertise

Demonstrate Knowledge : Share your expertise through detailed posts, articles, and videos. This positions you as a thought leader in your field.

Example :

"Finance professionals can share market analyses and investment tips, demonstrating their deep industry knowledge."

5. Leverage Visual Content

Use Multimedia : Incorporate videos, infographics, and high-quality images to make your content more engaging and accessible.

Example :

"Gary Vaynerchuk leverages video content extensively, providing valuable insights in a dynamic format."

Conclusion

Recap of Key Points : Summary of the Most Important Strategies Discussed

As we wrap up this comprehensive guide to mastering LinkedIn, let's recap the key strategies that will help you maximize your professional presence on the platform :

1. Crafting a Compelling Profile

- Use a professional and approachable profile picture.

- Write a clear, keyword-rich headline and an engaging summary.

- Regularly update your work experience, skills, and accomplishments.

2. Building and Engaging Your Network

- Connect with industry professionals and alumni.

- Participate in LinkedIn groups and discussions.

- Consistently share valuable content and engage with your connections' posts.

3. Showcasing Skills and Endorsements

- Select relevant skills that highlight your strengths.

- Actively seek and give endorsements.

- Request and provide detailed, specific recommendations.

4. Content Creation and Sharing

- Identify your audience and create valuable, relevant content.

- Use a mix of articles, videos, infographics, and posts.

- Maintain a consistent posting schedule and engage with your audience.

5. Leveraging Analytics and Advertising

- Monitor profile and content performance using LinkedIn analytics.

- Use data to refine your content and engagement strategies.

- Explore LinkedIn advertising options to reach a broader audience.

6. Optimizing Visual Elements

- Choose a high-quality profile picture and a professional banner image.

- Use AI tools like DALL-E and MidJourney for creating unique banner images.

- Ensure your visual elements align with your personal or company brand.

7. Learning from Success Stories

- Study the profiles of key personalities and influential users.

- Apply tailored advice for different industries.

- Extract key takeaways and lessons learned from successful LinkedIn users.

Taking Action : Encouragement and Next Steps for Readers to Implement the Guidance

Now that you've learned the strategies to optimize your LinkedIn presence, it's time to take action. Here's how to get started :

1. Review and Revamp Your Profile

- Take a critical look at your current LinkedIn profile. Update your headline, summary, work experience, and skills. Ensure your profile picture and banner image are professional and aligned with your brand.

2. Expand Your Network

- Start connecting with professionals in your industry, alumni, and thought leaders. Personalize your connection requests and join relevant LinkedIn groups to expand your reach.

3. Engage Consistently

- Commit to a regular posting schedule. Share valuable content, comment on others' posts, and engage in discussions. Building relationships is key to a strong LinkedIn presence.

4. Leverage Analytics

- Regularly check LinkedIn analytics to understand what's working and what's not. Use these insights to refine your content strategy and improve engagement.

5. Explore Advertising Options

- Consider LinkedIn advertising to amplify your reach. Start with small campaigns targeting specific audiences and adjust based on performance data.

6. Seek Feedback

- Ask colleagues, mentors, and peers to review your LinkedIn profile and provide feedback. Continuous improvement is essential for maintaining a strong presence.

Additional Resources : Suggestions for Further Reading and Tools

To further enhance your LinkedIn strategy, here are some additional resources and tools :

1. Books and Articles

- *LinkedIn Unlocked : Unlock the Mystery of LinkedIn To Drive More Sales Through Social Selling* by Melonie Dodaro

- *The LinkedIn Playbook : Contacts to Customers. Engage. Connect. Convert.* by Adam Houlahan

- LinkedIn's own *Help Center* and *Blog* for updates and tips.

2. Online Courses

- LinkedIn Learning : Courses on personal branding, LinkedIn strategy, and content creation.

- Coursera : *Digital Marketing Specialization* by the University of Illinois, which includes LinkedIn strategies.

3. Tools

- Canva : For creating visually appealing images and infographics.

- Hootsuite : For scheduling posts and tracking engagement across social media platforms.

- LinkedIn Sales Navigator : For advanced lead generation and networking.

- Grammarly : To ensure your LinkedIn content is free of grammatical errors.

4. AI Tools

- DALL-E : For generating creative and unique images for your profile and banner.

- MidJourney : For creating artistic and visually striking banner images.

Mastering LinkedIn is a continuous journey that involves regular updates, active engagement, and strategic content sharing. By implementing the strategies discussed in this guide, you can enhance your professional presence, build meaningful connections, and achieve your career goals. Remember, the key to LinkedIn success lies in consistency, authenticity, and ongoing learning. Start today by revamping your profile, engaging with your network, and sharing valuable insights. With dedication and the right approach, LinkedIn can be a powerful tool for your professional growth and success.

APPENDICES

LinkedIn Glossary : Definitions of Common LinkedIn Terms

1. Connection : A person with whom you have mutually agreed to share information on LinkedIn. Connections can be first-degree (direct connections), second-degree (connections of your first-degree connections), or third-degree (connections of your second-degree connections).

2. InMail : A LinkedIn feature that allows users to send messages to other LinkedIn members without needing to be connected.

3. LinkedIn Pulse : LinkedIn's publishing platform where users can write and share long-form content, such as articles and blog posts.

4. Endorsement : A feature that allows your connections to verify your skills listed on your profile, increasing your credibility.

5. Recommendation : A written statement from a LinkedIn member that endorses another member's professional skills and experience.

6. LinkedIn Learning : An online learning platform offering courses on various topics, including professional development and skills training.

7. LinkedIn Groups : Community spaces on LinkedIn where

members with similar interests or industries can share content, ask questions, and network.

8. LinkedIn Recruiter : A premium product designed for recruiters to find, connect with, and manage candidates.

9. LinkedIn Premium : A subscription service offering additional features such as InMail credits, advanced search filters, and detailed profile views.

10. Company Page : A dedicated page for a company or organization on LinkedIn, used to share updates, job postings, and company information.

11. LinkedIn Ads : Paid advertising on LinkedIn, including Sponsored Content, Sponsored InMail, Text Ads, and Dynamic Ads.

12. Analytics : Tools provided by LinkedIn to measure the performance of your profile, posts, and company pages, providing insights into engagement and reach.

13. Open to Work : A profile feature that signals to recruiters that you are open to job opportunities, often indicated by a photo frame on your profile picture.

14. Skills and Endorsements : Sections of your profile where you can list your professional skills, which can then be endorsed by your connections.

15. Thought Leader : A person recognized for their expertise and influence in a particular field, often sharing valuable insights and content on LinkedIn.

Templates and Checklists : Useful Templates for Profiles, Summaries, and Recommendations

Profile Template :

Headline :

- "Job Title | Key Skills | Industry Expertise"

Summary :

- "Experienced [Job Title] with [number] years in [Industry]. Skilled in [Skill 1], [Skill 2], and [Skill 3]. Passionate about [specific interest or goal]. Proven track record of [specific achievements]. Seeking to leverage my expertise in [specific role or opportunity]."

Experience :

- Job Title, Company Name, Dates of Employment

- Key Responsibilities :

 - [Responsibility 1]

 - [Responsibility 2]

- Key Achievements :

 - [Achievement 1 with metrics]

 - [Achievement 2 with metrics]

Skills :

- [Skill 1]

- [Skill 2]

- [Skill 3]

Education :

- Degree, Major, University Name, Graduation Year

Contact Information :

- Email : [Your Email]

- Phone : [Your Phone Number]

Summary Checklist :

- [ ] Clear and engaging opening statement

- [ ] Highlighted key skills and experiences

- [ ] Specific and measurable achievements

- [ ] Personal touch or unique selling point

- [ ] Call to action or professional goals

Recommendation Template :

Opening :

- "It is my pleasure to recommend [Name] for [specific role or opportunity]."

Body :

- "I had the opportunity to work with [Name] at [Company] where they served as [Job Title]. During this time, [Name] demonstrated exceptional skills in [Skill 1], [Skill 2], and [Skill 3]."

Achievements :

- "One of [Name]'s most notable achievements was [specific achievement with metrics]."

Closing :

- "I am confident that [Name] will continue to excel in [specific role or field]. I highly recommend [Name] for any opportunity that comes their way."

Signature :

- "[Your Name], [Your Job Title], [Your Company]"

Recommendation Checklist :

- [ ] Clear and specific opening statement
- [ ] Detailed description of the working relationship
- [ ] Highlighted key skills and experiences
- [ ] Specific achievements with measurable outcomes
- [ ] Strong closing endorsement

RESOURCES AND FURTHER READING : BOOKS, ARTICLES, AND WEBSITES FOR MORE INFORMATION

Books :

1. *LinkedIn Unlocked : Unlock the Mystery of LinkedIn To Drive More Sales Through Social Selling* by Melonie Dodaro

2. *The LinkedIn Playbook : Contacts to Customers. Engage. Connect. Convert.* by Adam Houlahan

3. *Crushing It! : How Great Entrepreneurs Build Their Business and Influence—and How You Can, Too* by Gary Vaynerchuk

4. *Optimize Your LinkedIn Profile : Get Connected to Recruiters and Land the Perfect Job* by Donna Serdula

Articles :

1. "10 Tips for Building a Strong LinkedIn Profile" - Harvard Business Review

2. "How to Use LinkedIn to Generate Leads" - Forbes

3. "LinkedIn Marketing : The Ultimate Guide" - HubSpot Blog

4. "Mastering LinkedIn Analytics : A Comprehensive Guide" - Sprout Social Blog

Websites :

1. LinkedIn Learning : [linkedin.com/learning](https : //www.linkedin.com/learning) - Offers courses on personal branding, LinkedIn strategies, and professional skills development.

2. LinkedIn Help Center : [linkedin.com/help](https : //www.linkedin.com/help) - Provides answers to common questions and tips for using LinkedIn effectively.

3. HubSpot Blog : [blog.hubspot.com](https : //blog.hubspot.com) - Offers comprehensive guides on LinkedIn marketing and optimization.

4. Social Media Examiner : [socialmediaexaminer.com](https : //www.socialmediaexaminer.com) - Features articles and tips on using LinkedIn for business growth and networking.

Tools :

1. Canva : [canva.com](https : //www.canva.com) - For creating visually appealing images, infographics, and banners.

2. Hootsuite : [hootsuite.com](https : //www.hootsuite.com) - For scheduling LinkedIn posts and tracking engagement metrics.

3. Grammarly : [grammarly.com](https : //www.grammarly.com) - For ensuring your LinkedIn content is free of grammatical errors.

4. Sales Navigator : [linkedin.com/sales/solutions/sales-navigator] (https : //www.linkedin.com/sales/solutions/sales-navigator)- For advanced lead generation and networking.

By utilizing these resources, templates, and checklists, you can continuously improve your LinkedIn profile and strategy, ensuring that you stay ahead in your professional journey.